The section on parakeet species contains full-color photos and descriptions, along with exact instructions on caring for the most popular species.

Please read the Important Note on page 95.

3

The World of Parakeets

Parakeets are extremely gregarious birds. In the wild, they often form a lifelong bond with a mate, with whom they then travel in groups or swarms. For this reason, in captivity they should be kept only in pairs or as a small flock. Keeping them singly is fundamentally inadvisable.

The world of parakeets is as varied and colorful as the plumage of these lively birds. Parakeets live in extremely diverse habitats throughout Australia and Asia and in the tropical and subtropical regions of Africa, Central America, and South America. Overall, there exist about 120 different species, many of which also have subspecies.

Habitats in the Wild

Most parakeets originally were forest dwellers. Because of their enormous adaptability, however, they also were able to settle in steppes, savannas, and deserts, along the courses of rivers, in cliffs or in the bush, and even in cities. Some parakeets live in mountains at an altitude of almost 10,000 feet (3000 m); others, such as the Antipodes Island green parakeet (*Cyanoramphus unicolor*), make their home—along with penguins—on an island at the edge of the Antarctic.

Parakeets Are Parrots Too

Parakeets belong to the parrot family, which is divided into several subfamilies within which the various parakeet genera are found. Externally, parakeets and parrots are hard to tell apart with certainty, although parakeets do tend to have a slender body with long tail feathers, while most parrots have a fairly compact build. (The shorter-tailed species, including the African parakeets, as well as the lories and lorikeets are not discussed in this volume.) In my opinion, you can tell one from another conclusively only by also taking into consideration the birds' habits. All parakeets are fast, agile,

tireless fliers; they are active and restless in the daytime. They cover fairly long distances by flying rapidly in a curved or undulating pattern, and some also fly straight as an arrow. By contrast, large parrots—Amazon parrots, for example—travel long distances in unhurried, soaring flight. When kept as cage or aviary birds, parakeets need to be housed and looked after very differently from parrots.

This book deals specifically with parakeets and their proper care.

External Features of Parakeets

Refer to page 85 for an illustration showing the external anatomy of parakeets.

The bill: Like parrots, parakeets have a hooked upper bill, or beak, that curves around the funnel-shaped lower bill. They use their bill and tongue to break up and peel fruits and seeds. The bill is also used to dig for food in the ground and to enlarge the entry hole and floor cavity of their nesting place. Parakeets use their bill to seize and hold fast to whatever object they are climbing, and in disputes they sometimes employ it for defense as well.

These young blue-winged parakeets already have begun to come to the entry hole to be fed. The time for them to leave the nest is not far off.

Annette Wolter

Long-Tailed Parakeets

How to Take Care of Them and Understand Them

With 50 color photos;
drawings by György Jankovics

Consulting Editor:
Matthew M. Vriends, Ph.D.

Contents

This Pennant's parakeet is taking the opportunity to bathe. It thrashes its wings vigorously to make sure that all parts of its body get wet.

2

The tongue: It is thick, round, and equipped with papillae for use in exploring and tasting. Parakeets can hull seeds easily with the aid of their tongue.

The cere: It is located at the top of the upper part of the beak and surrounds the nostrils. In most parakeet species the cere is unfeathered; often it is colorfully tinted.

The foot: The positioning of the toes makes the foot an excellent prehensile organ. Parakeets have two toes that point forward and two that point backward. They are particularly well-suited for grasping branches, clasping food, clinging to objects, and climbing.

The feathers: The plumage, which usually is brilliantly colored, serves as camouflage for parakeets. This may sound contradictory, but a brightly colored bird hunting for food in a sea of blossoms will scarcely be noticeable there. Many feather colors are adapted to the soil of a particular bird's habitat or appear in sunlight to be reflections in the leaves of the treetops. Differently colored areas of the plumage also play a role in courtship and in the life of the flock.

Typical Characteristics

Lifelong fidelity: Most parakeets are monogamous (see Glossary); that is, they form a lasting relationship with a mate of the opposite sex and remain faithful as long as they live. They may, however, also become attached to a bird of the same sex, or accept a different species as a mate, or even become devoted to a human as a substitute for a mate. Never separate a pair unless you have good reasons: The birds would suffer from the separation; their health would begin to fail, or they would become dejected. Only continual quarrels between the two

birds should give you cause to separate them.

Life expectancy: We know the life expectancy of only a few kinds of parakeets. Certainly they live longer in captivity than in the wild, where many kinds of dangers loom. A cautious estimate: Small parakeets, such as the budgerigar, Bourke's parakeet, and elegant parakeet, can live for ten years, while larger species, such as the regent parakeet and ringneck parakeet, may reach the age of 25.

Intelligence: The intellectual capacity of parakeets has not been observed as closely as that of the large parrots. From living with budgerigars and cockatiels, however, I know that they often amaze me with their strikingly intelligent behavior, such as the accomplishment of enormous feats of memory. If parakeets are kept in a pair or in a small flock in an aviary, however, their life revolves exclusively around their relationship with each other.

Vocalizations: Each parakeet species has its own calls to communicate with each other when flying or giving a warning. When searching for food, parakeets use location songs, or answering songs, to keep in contact with others of their kind. During periods of rest they sometimes chat together, twittering softly. When excited, however, they scream loudly and piercingly, and these noises can be quite unpleasant to the human ear. Keep in mind that the noise of a flock of parakeets may be a source of considerable annoyance to neighbors. (See Disturbance of the Peace in Glossary.)

Mimicry: In parakeets, the inclination and ability to mimic sounds vary widely. In captivity, many parakeets—without prompting—will imitate sounds that they hear in their environment. Some also repeat words or short sen-

A well-matched pair of parakeets should not be separated, because the birds would suffer greatly. Only in extremely rare cases would they be prepared to establish a new bond. Separate pairs only if they quarrel incessantly.

Male and female Nanday parakeets, or black-headed conures, cannot be told apart.

tences; others are gifted musicians and enjoy whistling their acquired repertoire. Birds in aviaries are known on occasion to mimic the melodies of our native songbirds.

Parakeets as Housemates

Basic needs: All parakeets have an inherent need for companionship, sufficient room to fly, an opportunity to climb, and plant matter to chew. They reach sexual maturity between the ages of five and thirty months, and at this time they experience a strong desire to mate and raise young.

Keeping a single bird: Basically, you should keep a single parakeet only if you spend the bulk of your time at home and are truly prepared to

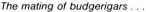
The mating of budgerigars . . .   *is sometimes a balancing act.*

substitute as the bird's full-time companion. A single parakeet needs a great deal of attention in the form of play, activity, and affection from "its" human; otherwise, it will waste away. Even if you meet these prerequisites, you should be fully aware that having a single parakeet is not in keeping with the needs of the species, because the bird cannot act in full accordance with its innate fundamental needs. It can never move around in a flock with others of its kind or form a permanent bond with a mate of its choosing.

Keeping a pair: If you want a pair of parakeets, make sure both birds are young when you buy them. (See What to Look for When You Buy, page 23.) Then they will learn easily to accept you as a member of the flock. If you choose birds of the same sex, you can avoid possibly undesira-

ble problems. If the birds bear young, space will be an issue, and sooner or later your flock will have to move into an aviary.

Parakeets Need Room

If you want to observe the typical life of a parakeet species and possibly also breed young birds, it is best to house your pets in a spacious aviary that offers the birds enough room to fly. This is a costly investment, however. A sufficiently large, safe aviary is expensive, needs a great deal of maintenance, and often requires—particularly if you want to build an outdoor aviary—a permit from local authorities and the consent of your neighbors. (See Outdoor Aviary, page 14.)

If an aviary is to be installed indoors, it should be located in a sufficiently large, bright room with screens on the windows. Put an aviary in an attic or a cellar only if the attic story or basement area has undergone extensive improvement and has plenty of light.

If you keep one or two parakeets in a cage, keep in mind that even the largest cage is not adequate as the birds' sole habitat. In their natural surroundings, parakeets are accustomed to cover large distances each day in their search for food or suitable places to sleep. Consequently, cage birds absolutely must be given an opportunity to fly around indoors for several hours every day. Let the parakeets fly free only under your supervision, however, because they occasionally nibble on furniture and walls and they can encounter indoor hazards. (See the table on page 31.)

Ten Points to Help You Decide

1. Are you and your family prepared to accept responsibility for the life and well-being of parakeets, which can live 10 to 20 years and more?

2. Is anyone in your family allergic to the dust from a parakeet's feathers? (See Important Note, page 95.)

3. Do you have other pets—cats, for example—that might harm the parakeets?

4. Who will take care of the birds if you are unable to do so? If you plan a vacation trip, you will have to arrange for a dependable caretaker in advance.

5. Parakeets need to be given fresh food and water at least once a day.

6. The food has to be procured on a regular basis, and is a regular expense.

7. The cage, aviary, and all objects with which the birds come in contact have to be kept clean, and this work is time-consuming.

8. An aviary—an outdoor aviary with a night shelter that can be

One broods, the other brings food.

heated—takes up room and is an expensive investment.

9. If you breed parakeets, keep in mind that you are allowed to sell young birds only if their species is not subject to trade prohibitions. (See Species Conservation, page 24.)

10. If the birds should ever need medical treatment, it can be expensive.

Appropriate Housing

The higher the perches are attached in an aviary, the more welcome they will be. Parakeets feel protected and safe when they sit and sleep high above the ground. Make sure to leave enough room at the top, so that the birds' heads do not bump against the roof.

The Right Cage

Size: For smaller parakeet species—for two budgerigars, for example—the cage needs to be 39 inches (100 cm) long, 20 inches (50 cm) wide, and 32 inches (80 cm) high. For larger species, such as two cockatiels, it should be 59 inches (150 cm) long, 32 inches (80 cm) wide, and 59 inches (150 cm) high. In general, this rule applies: The larger the cage, the happier your parakeets will be.

Important: Round cages are not suitable for parakeets.

Bars: The bars should run horizontally on at least two sides of the cage, so that the parakeets can climb on them. For small species the bars should be ½ inch (12 mm) apart; for larger ones, ¾ inch (20 mm).

The cage door: It has to be large enough for you to take the bird out while it sits on your hand. The lock or latch on the door must be "beak-proof."

The bottom pan: It should be made of impact-resistant heatproof plastic and be equipped with a sliding sand tray or drawer. If there is a floor grate (see Glossary) over the sand drawer, remove it, because parakeets like to pick grit and tiny stones—which aid in digestion—out of the sand.

Food dishes: The two food dishes that come with the cage are not enough. Buy two or three additional, larger dishes made of high-grade steel that can be attached to the side of the cage. They are the easiest to keep clean, and they will continue to look attractive for years.

The Indoor Aviary

Indoor aviaries for parakeets are available in different styles and sizes in pet stores. The ideal size is about 47 × 32 × 67 inches (120 × 80 × 170 cm). A cage this large can accommodate two pairs of a smaller species—budgerigars, Bourke's parakeets, or elegant parakeets—assuming they are given a chance each day to fly free outside the cage under your supervision.

Indoor aviaries with prefabricated components are also available. The parts can be put together easily to form an indoor aviary of any size you desire. An aviary of this kind can be built in a corner of a room, with the walls of the room forming two sides of the enclosure. If you allow about 21.5 square feet 2 m² per bird, the parakeets will not need to fly free outside the aviary.

Aviary room: If you have enough space available, you can even equip an entire room as an aviary. (See Proper Equipment for Aviaries and Cages, page 15.)

Pointer: The wider and longer an indoor aviary is, the happier your parakeets will feel in it. Long-distance fliers such as the Psephotus species are not suited for keeping in an indoor aviary, because they always require a great deal of flying space.

The red-capped parakeet lives primarily on the seed pods of eucalyptus fruits. To hull these pods, this parakeet species has developed a special beak shape: The upper bill is longer and less hooked.

This red-capped parakeet is paying close attention to what is happening around it.

HOW-TO
Equipment

On these pages you will find important items of equipment that should be placed in every aviary. A climbing tree, for example, is a wonderful place for your parakeets to play and enjoy themselves. It will provide them with ideal places to land, rest, and sleep. In addition, I recommend that in roomy aviaries you mount a feeding shelf on the wall. The dishes will not slide around there, and the parakeets can reach their food comfortably.

The Bird Tree

You can buy a bird tree in a pet store, but with a modicum of skill you also can construct one yourself. The larger it is, the more your parakeets will enjoy spending time there. From time to time you will have to replace branches that the birds have gnawed. Even the trunk may have to be replaced.

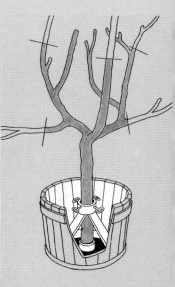

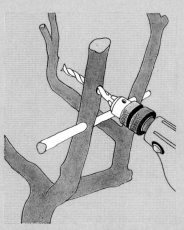

2 | Bore holes in the tree branches for additional branch perches.

3 | Add large rocks, gravel, soil, and bird sand to the tub.

Drawing 2
Take the trunk out of the tub again and, using a drill, bore holes in the branches. Insert additional branches into the holes and tie them securely with tear-resistant twine.

1 | Saw off any branches that jut out over the side of the tub.

Drawing 1
From friends with a yard or garden—or when trees are being trimmed in a city park—get a strong piece of a tree limb with many branches or a small tree that has been cut down. First put it in a Christmas tree stand, then place it in a large plastic or wooden tub. Next saw off any branches that extend beyond the tub, so that no bird droppings will fall outside it.

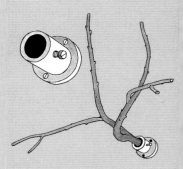

4 | Attach the branches to the wall (wire mesh) with branch mounts.

Drawing 3

Now return the climbing tree in its stand to the tub and weight it with large rocks. Then place a layer of coarse gravel in the tub, cover it with a layer of soil, and finally, pour bird sand on top.

The feeding shelf can be fastened to a wall or to the side of the cage.

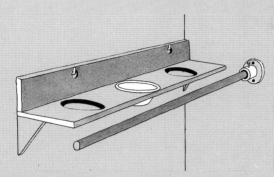

Pointer: Don't put drinking water on the feeding shelf; the parakeets would also bathe in it and splash water on the food.

Drawing 5

Get a sturdy board long enough to hold three or four food dishes. To keep the dishes from sliding around, shape indentations in the board or cut out holes in which the dishes can be set. Next, fasten the shelf to the wall or the wire mesh of the aviary. In front of the shelf, attach a perch on which the birds can land. Use a branch mount to attach the perch to the wall or the mesh. Do not put a perch above the shelf: the food would be contaminated by bird droppings.

My tip: Feeding shelves made of plastic or metal grating also can be bought ready-made in pet stores.

Drawing 6

The feeding shelf also can be suspended in the aviary. Let it hang from two chains or wire cables attached to the ceiling, but near enough to a side wall to mount a perch next to it for the birds to land on.

5 | The feeding shelf should be long enough to hold at least three food dishes.

Branch Mounts

Drawing 4

The branches used as perches for sitting and sleeping should be fastened securely to the wall or the aviary mesh. Special branch mounts for this purpose are available in various sizes in pet stores.

The Feeding Shelf

If you have a cage or a small indoor aviary, simply hang the food dishes on the side of the bars. If you have a relatively large indoor aviary or an outdoor aviary, I recommend that you install a feeding shelf. In an outdoor aviary, it is best to put the feeding shelf inside the shelter or in the covered portion of the flight area.

In order to save space, the feeding shelf also can be hung from chains attached to the roof.

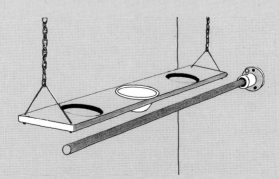

6 | Attach an approach branch in front of the shelf, so that the birds can reach their food easily.

A yellow-fronted parakeet taking a sunbath. This species likes to spend time on the ground at other times too.

Outdoor Aviary

There are as many ways to build an aviary in your yard as to design a house for a family. Before you start to build an aviary yourself or hire someone to do the job, obtain as much information as possible (see Useful Addresses and Literature, page 95). It is also a good idea to contact breeders and other people who keep birds, because from their experience you can glean tips that will not appear in any textbook. On page 18 you will find a list of important points to keep in mind when building an outdoor aviary.

Before Construction Begins, Settle These Issues:

- What official permits are required for your aviary? To build an outdoor aviary you often need a building permit.
- Do your neighbors approve the project? Many parakeet species have extremely loud voices. To prevent trouble later, don't keep your plans a secret.

- What species of parakeet do you ntend to keep, and how many birds do you want?
- If you are interested primarily in watching the birds, it is best to build the aviary near the house in your line of vision. If you are chiefly interested n breeding parakeets, put the aviary n a quiet corner of the yard, because brooding parakeets want to be disturbed as little as possible.
- Connections for electricity and water should be available in an outdoor aviary.
- For winter, parakeets need a night shelter that can be heated, because most species come from tropical regions.
- Ideally, the front side of the aviary should face southeast or southwest, so that plenty of sunlight is available.
- Some protection from the sun, wind, and rain has to be provided in an outdoor aviary.
- You may have to isolate individual birds that, despite all precautionary measures, are quarrelsome and dangerous to the other inhabitants of the aviary. For this purpose, you will need to create one or two smaller compartments within the aviary. Use double wire mesh to separate these compartments from the large common area.
- If you intend to breed parakeets, each breeding pair will need its own compartment in the aviary flight (the large enclosed area where the birds can fly about) and in the night shelter.
- An extra room in the night shelter— ideally, with a connection to the water mains—is very useful for storing food to keep it safe from pests and for housing all the equipment used to keep the aviary clean.

Proper Equipment for Aviaries and Cages

The following suggestions for appropriate furnishings are applicable to all aviaries and cages.

Perches: Replace the dowel perches that come with the cage or aviary with natural branches of various diameters ($7/16$ to $9/16$ [12 to 14 mm]). The variation in size will allow the birds to exercise their feet in a natural way. In a cage, the branches can be fixed in place by making notches near the ends and fitting them on the bars. In addition, tie them on securely with strong twine. In an aviary, branch perches can easily be attached to the wire mesh or the wall by means of special branch mounts (see drawing 4 on page 12).

How many branch perches? One branch has to be attached in front of the food dishes so that the birds can reach the food comfortably. A second branch to serve as a place to sleep needs to be large enough for a pair, and it should be placed as high as possible, but not so high that the birds' heads touch the ceiling. Parakeets always choose the highest branch for sleeping, because they feel safest there. In an outdoor aviary, attach the sleeping branches in the night shelter, and place them higher than the branches in the flight. Make sure that the parakeets' freedom of movement is not restricted by the presence of too many branch perches.

Where to get natural branches: Pet stores sell natural branches. Many people who have gardens also will give away branches after they prune their trees. Before using any branch, scrub it thoroughly under hot running water to remove any harmful residues.

Suitable woods: Maple, birch, willow, apple, pear, beech, oak, ash, elm, walnut.

The branch perches in the cage, in the aviary, or on the bird tree have to be thick enough to keep the front and back of the parakeets' claws from touching when their toes wrap around the wood. Don't use metal perches; they are inappropriate for parakeets.

Caution: Laburnum (*Cytisus laburnum*), acacia (*Robinia*), yew, rhododendron, boxwood, buckthorn, cherry (*Prunus* spp.), horse chestnut, privet, and oleander branches are poisonous!

Parakeets like to gnaw: Parakeets' strong urge to chew can be satisfied only if the birds have plant matter available at all times. Offer them bundles of twigs (see drawing, left), knotted hemp rope, cuttlebone or mineral blocks, and small unplaned boards of soft natural wood (elder, chestnut, linden, poplar, and willow branches; fruit tree branches, provided they have not been sprayed with chemicals).

Moisture for Plumage

Parakeets need access to water for bathing or "showering" at all times. Moisture keeps their plumage healthy and makes it glossy and attractive (see also Atmospheric humidity, page 22). In the wild, many species prefer to use bodies of standing water for bathing. When kept as pets, consequently, they need appropriate water containers. Other species do not bathe; instead, they enjoy letting themselves be sprinkled by the rain. As a substitute for this pleasure, you can moisten their feathers with a plant sprayer. In the profiles on pages 64 through 81 you will find information on the type of bath preferred by each parakeet species.

Bathhouse: If your parakeets live in a cage, hang a little bathhouse (various sizes are available in pet stores) in the open door of the cage.

Bathing dishes: Aviary birds can use a shallow bowl filled with water. It is best to set it on a small pedestal so that the water does not get dirty so quickly. For smaller species, a large earthenware flowerpot saucer will work nicely. For larger species, use a large container made of plastic (a cat litter box, for example) or a birdbath made

of stone, large enough to be filled to a depth of about 2 inches (5 cm).

Pointer: During the winter months when the parakeets are housed in the night shelter, the container can be placed on a special hot plate (from a pet store). Do not use a plastic container! Put the cord and the hot plate where the birds cannot reach them!

Important: Wash all bathing dishes daily and fill them with fresh water, because the birds also drink from them.

Spray bottle for misting plants: If your parakeets like taking a spray bath, sprinkle them two or three times a week from a distance of about 6½ feet (2 m).

Caution: Make sure the spray bottle has never contained pesticides, fertilizer, or other chemicals.

Dew bath: Many parakeets greatly enjoy dampening their feathers with water from a bunch of wet herbs, which can be fastened to a branch perch.

Shower corner: You can install a shower in a corner of an indoor aviary or in a room used as an aviary (see drawing, page 35).

Sprinkler: A rotating sprinkler, fixed securely in its place, is ideal for all parakeets that live in an outdoor aviary. The sprinkler can be turned on and off via a water faucet.

Room Ventilation and Lighting

Whether the area in question is a cage, an indoor aviary, or a night shelter in an outdoor aviary, it must be possible for sufficient air to circulate there without creating drafts.

I recommend that you put screens on the windows of the room where you keep your parakeets, so that the windows can be opened safely. The birds will be able to enjoy fresh air at all times during the warm season. During the cold months of the year, you also will need to open the windows slightly from time to time so that enough fresh air can circulate.

Parakeets like to gnaw on fresh twigs and herbs. Ideally, suspend a bundle of twigs by a short piece of twine attached to a branch. Alternatively, fasten the twigs to the wire mesh of the cage with a wooden clothespin.

16

The red mask of this parakeet species spreads out to form spots on the bird's forehead, crown, lore, cheeks, and ear coverts. Many birds also have individual red feathers distributed over their entire body.

The mitred conure's powerful bill comes in handy when the bird preens its feathers.

17

HOW-TO
Outdoor Aviary

Before you start to build an outdoor aviary with a night shelter, obtain all the necessary permits (see page 14).

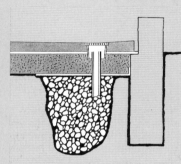

1|A cross section showing the foundation, floor, and drain.

When Building an Outdoor Aviary

• Construct the aviary so solidly that rodents like mice, rats, or weasels cannot make their way in. They transmit diseases and may attack the birds.
• Usually only one parakeet species can live in a community aviary (see Drawing 3). For several species, you will need a larger structure known as a birdroom, an aviary complex with individual compartments (see Drawing 4).
• For the best results, construct the foundation, floor, and frame as shown in Drawings 1 and 2.
• The wooden and metal parts of the aviary and the wire mesh must be given a coat of protec-

tive paint. For this purpose, use only nontoxic synthetic resin-based coatings!
• Cover a portion of the flight with a roof so that the birds can move into the shade at any time.
• Depending on the location, the climate, and the parakeet species, use wall components to create a corner in the aviary sheltered from the wind.

Foundation and Floor
Drawing 1

The foundation (poured concrete or brickwork) should be 4 inches (10 cm) wide and extend to a depth of 32 inches (80 cm) below ground level.

A drain is necessary so that rainwater can run off. Dig the hole 28 to 32 inches (70–80 cm) deep. Put in a layer of 3- to 16-millimeter gravel about 16 inches (40 cm) deep, and set the drainpipe in it so that it later will be flush with the concrete floor. Then fill the hole to the top with gravel and cover it with tar paper.

Capillary layer: Put down a layer of gravelly filler sand. On top of it lay a sheet of waterproof plastic, then a mat of wire fabric.

Floor: Pour the concrete floor so that it slopes down into the drainage hole. Between the concrete floor and the foundation, attach an expansion joint all around, using styrofoam ⅖ inch (1 cm) thick. Cover the floor with a layer of soil or sand, which will be easy to replace.

Pointer: If you decide to have a dirt floor instead of a concrete slab: Dig down about 16 inches (40 cm), then cover the ground completely, leaving

no gaps, with plastic netting (mesh size ⁵⁄₁₆ to ½ inch [10–13 mm]), so that no pests can enter the aviary from underground. On top of this netting, put a drainage layer (mixture of sand and gravel) about 8 inches (20 cm) deep, followed by a layer of topsoil, which absolutely must be removed and replaced twice a year to prevent infestations of worms and keep out disease-causing organisms.

Frame and Wire Mesh
There are two possibilities:
1. Use ready-made components—metal frames already covered with wire mesh.
2. Construct it yourself, using squared lengths of wood (3 × 3 inches [8 × 8 cm]) to which you attach spot-welded galvanized wire mesh (1 millimeter). Two layers of mesh are best (see Drawing 2) because they will give better protection from cats and thieves: inner face (mesh no more than ⅖ inch [1 cm]); outer face (mesh somewhat larger).

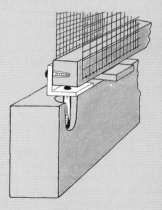

2|The wooden frame is fastened to the base with corner brackets.

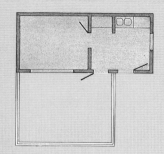

3|Sketch of a community aviary with an anteroom.

My tip: If aggressive species are neighbors in your aviary (*Platycercus* species), by all means use double mesh for the dividing walls. Even better, don't put such species in proximity.

Attaching the Wooden Frame
Drawing 2
Using plastic dowels, connect the frame to the concrete base with corner brackets. Place small pieces of wood ⅖ inch (1 cm) thick between the frame and the base. Remove them once the aviary is completed.

Community Aviary
Drawing 3
A community aviary consists of a flight, a night shelter, and an anteroom with a connection to the water mains, to serve as a storeroom for all the equipment needed in cleaning the aviary. You also can isolate a sick parakeet there from its fellow birds. The anteroom should have access to both the night shelter and the flight.

Birdroom
Drawing 4
If you want to breed several species of parakeets, you need to provide each pair with its own compartment in the aviary and in the night shelter. Birdrooms based on the plan illustrated here (see Drawing 4) have proved reliable.

The Night Shelter
The parakeets will spend the winter in the night shelter, where a temperature comfortable for the birds should be maintained constantly (cool in summer, about 46°F [8°C] in winter). Specialized books (see page 95) will provide you with exact information on building a night shelter.

When Planning, Remember These Points:
• The night shelter needs a solid foundation and, ideally, a concrete floor.
• The walls and ceiling must be insulated.
• The roof has to be sturdy enough to withstand storms, hail, and the weight of snow.
• Water and electricity (for lighting and heating) must be available.
• On the side of the night shelter that faces the aviary put windows with wired glass. They are sturdy and will help the birds recognize the glass as a barrier that restricts their movement.
• Above the windows in every compartment make a hole for entry and exit, with a flap or door that can be closed. So that you will not have to enter the flight, you should be able to open and shut the door from the feeding corridor with a length of wire cable.
• In a birdroom, use fiberboard or stone walls to build the partitions inside the night shelter, so that the birds can have some privacy.

My tip: During the cold part of the year, the night shelter can be heated as necessary with small heaters and automatic frost controllers (500 W/ 220 V).

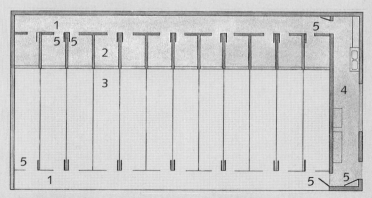

4|Birdroom and flight: 1 feeding corridor and "lock," or safety area; 2 compartment in shelter; 3 compartment in flight; 4 anteroom; 5 door.

19

Pennant's parakeets in the wild, shown here bathing and drinking at a watering site. Like all *Platycercus* species, they need opportunity to bathe whenever they choose. If they are kept as cage or aviary birds, they will also be happy with a shallow bowl of water. It is important that fresh, clean water be available.

After every meal, parakeets sharpen their beak on a branch perch to clean it and keep it in trim. (Drawing: Cockatiel)

Atmospheric humidity: For the well-being of most parakeet species, a humidity level of 60 to 70 percent is essential. A few days before the young hatch, a level of 80 percent is necessary. If the air is too dry, the birds' feathers will become dull and lusterless, and the dust in their feathers will cause itching. You can use a hygrometer to measure the humidity and, as necessary, a humidifier to increase the level of moisture in the air (both available from specialized dealers and pet stores).

Lighting: Most parakeets live in parts of the world where day and night are of equal length. The short days of our winter months are stressful for these natives of the tropics. In addition, the amount of available daylight—after it is filtered through window glass—is often adequate. Particularly in rooms with poor light, provide sufficient brightness 12 hours a day with artificial lighting. It is best if the light goes on and off gradually, regulated by an automatic dimmer switch, to simulate dawn and dusk. Then the birds will not be startled in the morning when the light comes on, and in the evening they can find their sleeping place as twilight falls. Use only lights whose color spectrum corresponds to that of daylight.

Pointer: Install the lighting so that the cords are out of the birds' reach; otherwise, they will nibble on them. (See Useful Addresses and Literature, page 95.)

Tips on Plants for the Aviary

Plants in an aviary are not only attractive, but also functional. They provide parakeets with perching sites and plenty of privacy and cover. Many plants—such as chickweed and potherbs—also are suitable as additional food. Because the birds nibble at the plants with their bills, it is advisable to use only inexpensive plants that grow rapidly. Of course, they also have to be nonpoisonous (see Poisonous Plants in Glossary).

My tip: Preferably, buy two identical sets of plants. Then you can replace badly gnawed plants and give the damaged ones a chance to recover.

Pointer: Cover the soil surrounding plants in tubs or pots with fine-meshed wire netting, so that the birds do not touch the soil. It might contain pathogenic organisms or artificial fertilizers that can cause diseases in birds.

Ground covers of grass or wild plants are popular with those parakeet species (*Neophema* species, for example) that like to dig in the ground with their beaks and eat grass.

The surroundings of the outdoor aviary also can be planted in a practical way. Shrubs such as members of the genus *Cornus*, hazelnut (*Corylus*), and elder (*Sambucus nigra*) keep off wind and rain on the windward side, and deciduous trees provide shade on the sunny side. These plantings, however, should not block too much light.

22

Tips on Buying a Parakeet

Where to Get Parakeets

Pet stores have parakeets for sale, and they often can obtain for you the species you want. The pet store dealer also will give you addresses of breeders who specialize in certain species. Specialized periodicals (see page 95) always contain breeders' advertisements.

My tip: Most parakeets breed during the summer, and by fall the young are on their own. If possible, contact several breeders in summer, discuss your wishes with them, keep the species you have chosen under close scrutiny, and arrange to buy a bird from a breeder in the fall.

Considerations Before You Buy

Keeping a pair: If you want pairs of parakeets, keep in mind that each breeding pair needs its own compartment in the aviary and in the night shelter. Buy two or three young males and two or three young females of each species that you want to keep. Then put all the birds of each species in a common compartment. This way they have a chance to make their own matches, even before the onset of puberty. If some of the birds are not ready to form part of a couple, try asking the breeder to exchange the loners for other birds. An exchange is possible, however, only if it was agreed upon expressly in the sales contract (see page 26).

If you want to keep a pair in an indoor aviary or in a large cage, I recommend that you choose two birds of the same sex if you are not interested in breeding. A male and a female that go through the process of pair formation ought to be given a chance to breed. The following species are especially well-suited for keeping in pairs in an indoor aviary: budgerigars, cockatiels, Bourke's parakeets, Stanley parakeets, red-fronted New Zealand parakeets, and *Psephotus haematogaster*.

A parakeet flock: Parakeets of a single species generally live together in a community aviary. Particularly peaceable species suitable for keeping in a small group are the following: the regent parakeet, superb parakeet, red-fronted New Zealand parakeet, and princess parakeet. Cockatiels, budgerigars, and Bourke's parakeets are species that also get along well in a common aviary. Red-fronted New Zealand parakeets can also live together with red-rumped parakeets. Buy either exclusively males or exclusively females. Alternatively, if you are willing to have them produce offspring, buy equal numbers of males and females. Allow 21½ square feet (2 m²) of space per bird.

What to Look for When You Buy

• I suggest that you buy only young parakeets, because only young birds will settle in quickly, form pairs readily, and be less quarrelsome. For a beginner, however, it is difficult to tell whether a parakeet is still young. In many species the young birds have shorter tails, paler plumage colors, or eyes whose irises differ in color from those of mature birds. Here it is best to place your trust in an experienced

If you have no experience in keeping and breeding parakeets, it is best to start by taking care of a pair or a fairly small group of budgerigars or cockatiels. These two species are extremely peaceable, develop trust easily, and breed readily.

Even if the breeder or pet store is far away, always pick up your parakeets yourself. Shipping them is cruel to the birds. Moreover, you will have a chance to assess the parakeets' previous accommodations and the state of their health before you buy the birds.

and reputable pet store dealer or breeder.
• Make sure that the parakeet is wearing a closed, not an open, leg band (see How-To, page 55). Then you can be certain that the band was put on the bird while it was a nestling and that the bird really is young (its year of birth appears on the leg band).
• If you plan to breed the birds, make sure that each of the young parakeets comes from different pairs of parents, not related to each other. It is best to buy each bird from a different breeder in order to rule out the possibility of inbreeding.
• If you intend to breed pure varieties, never buy hybrids (see Mutation in Glossary). Many parakeet species are endangered, and for this reason they should remain as nature created them.
• Many young birds can be sexed only after they reach puberty. In some species, the sex cannot be determined by external features. Only a surgical procedure (see Endoscopy in Glossary) could tell for certain. Nonetheless, experienced breeders often know the sex of their young birds. If it turns out, however, that you have bought a male instead of a female or vice versa, you have the right to return the bird only if its gender was specified in the contract of sale (see page 26).

How to Recognize a Healthy Parakeet
• All the feathers are fully formed and not stuck together. The bird has no unfeathered spots. Plumage that is somewhat the worse for wear may be left from the bird's nestling phase. After the first molt, it will be normal.
• The feathers surrounding the cloaca—this is the term used for a bird's anus—are not smeared with feces.

• Two toes of each foot point to the front and two to the back. All the toes have claws. The absence of a toe or a claw is not necessarily an indication of disease. A male that you plan to breed, however, should have all its toes; otherwise, it cannot hold fast to the female's back during the mating act (see page 58).
• The droppings consist of soft white excrement (urine) and moderately firm, black or dark green excrement (feces).
• The eyes are clear, the lids are not stuck together, and the nostrils are not producing any discharge.
• The bill has the typical shape of a parakeet's bill (see Glossary). If the horny substance of the bill is slightly splintered at the edges, this is normal; the bill is continually regenerated in this way.

Important Information on Species Conservation
The Convention on International Trade in Endangered Species (CITES) regulates the protection of species of animals and plants that are threatened worldwide. Depending on the degree to which they require protection, parrots—which, of course, include parakeets—were placed in conservation categories I and II. Parrots that are threatened with extinction are listed in Appendix I. Trade in these species is no longer permitted; they may be neither bought nor sold. This embargo applies even if the birds have been bred in captivity. All other parrots are listed in Appendix II (with the exception of the cockatiel, the ringneck parakeet, and the budgerigar, which are not subject to species conservation restrictions). Trade in category II species is permitted if the legal regulations are observed. This also applies to captive-bred birds. You can buy parakeets sold in pet stores with an easy mind, provided the bird is wear-

The gray-cheeked or orange-flanked parakeet owes the second of its common names to the brilliant orange color seen here.

ing the leg band prescribed by law and you obtain the necessary CITES certificate.

Pointer: In the case of captive-bred parakeets, the authorities sometimes will exempt birds from the trade restrictions.

Formalities at the Time of Purchase

The CITES certificate: As the owner of a protected species of parakeet, you have to furnish proof of legal ownership. The so-called CITES certificate, which constitutes such proof, is given to you—already filled out—when you buy each parakeet. Do not buy or sell any parakeet without this document and the official leg band.

The leg band: According to law, every parakeet that comes from a licensed quarantine station must be given the required metal or plastic leg band with a number stamped on it (see How-To, page 55). This law was enacted because of psittacosis (see page 46); today, however, the disease no longer presents any significant threat. The leg band attests to the bird's origin in a healthy bird population and, in case of illness, makes it possible to ascertain the bird's breeder. In addition, if an escaped parakeet is wearing a leg band, its owner can be ascertained easily.

The sales contract: Every well-run pet store and every conscientious breeder will provide the purchaser with a detailed certificate of sale. This contract should provide the following information: the date of sale, the bird's species or subspecies, the number on the leg band, the age and—if it can be determined—the sex of the parakeet, and the addresses of the buyer and seller.

When a parakeet sleeps, it sticks its bill into its back feathers and often draws up one leg into the feathers on the abdomen. (Drawing: Turquoise parakeet)

Pointer: If you are party to the acquisition of a bird through a trade or loan, as a gift, or via a breeders' association, make every effort to see that the written agreements are as explicit as the contract of sale.

Compulsory registration: An owner is required to report without delay the possession of any parakeet (except cockatiels, budgerigars, and ringneck parakeets) to the appropriate wildlife conservation authority. You must provide all the information contained in the sales contract, in addition to the location of the aviary, the purpose for which the bird is to be used, and the registration number of the CITES certificate.

Transport

To ensure that you bring healthy, lively birds into your house, I strongly suggest that you yourself pick up the parakeets from the pet store or breeder, no matter how far you have to travel. It would be cruel to make a bird travel in a container by public transportation.

Transport cage: If the parakeets do not know each other, each will need its own transport container for the trip, because there is some danger of their injuring one another. Nest siblings or pairs on intimate terms can be transported together in a single container. You can buy a special transport cage in a pet store or borrow one from the breeder. Protect the birds from cold, heat, and dampness and bring them to their new accommodations via the quickest route.

Acclimation, Care, and Hygiene

Let all the parakeets that are going to live in a community move into their new quarters at the same time. If you cannot buy all the birds at one time, let the first few parakeets spend the intervening time in separate cages, waiting until all the birds are assembled. Particularly peaceable species like budgerigars, Bourke's parakeets, or regent parakeets can, if need be, also be put in common cages, two to each cage.

Moving into an Aviary

Community aviary: Put the parakeets into the outdoor aviary shelter or the indoor aviary together, in the morning if possible. This will ensure that none of the birds has any kind of preferential claim; all of them are as yet strangers to each other and equally unsure in their new surroundings. They will get used to each other quickly and divide up the area among themselves. Full food and water dishes should be already on hand. If the birds are in the shelter of an outdoor aviary, you can open the entry and exit door the next morning to let the birds inspect the flight as well. Full food and water dishes should be in readiness there ahead of time. Then you will not need to disturb the birds by entering the flight during the early hours of the day.

Aviary compartment: Birds also should move into an aviary compartment together. The various compartments can be occupied progressively.

Pointer: During the first few days, you will have to check on the birds re-peatedly, so that you can intervene if quarrels flare up. Keep a bird net handy for such an eventuality, and if necessary remove a troublemaker and put it either in a vacant compartment or in a cage.

My tip: If you have never caught a bird with a net, be sure to have a breeder show you how to use it, so that the bird is not injured and does not escape.

Moving into a Cage

After you have equipped the cage and filled the food and water dishes, you can let your new parakeet or pair of parakeets into the new home. Watch the parakeets more closely than is necessary with an aviary; if quarrels erupt, the birds cannot avoid each other in the close confines of the cage.

Getting Parakeets Used to Each Other

These scenarios are common: New parakeets have to be integrated into an existing aviary community; a breeding pair has to be brought together; or your singly kept pet is going to be joined by a companion.

During your parakeets' acclimation, you will have to devote a great deal of time to them. Only by watching the birds virtually round the clock will you be able to intervene in time if serious quarrels erupt.

Moving into a Community Aviary

A new arrival often has a hard time holding its own against an established aviary community. The "old" parakeets consider the new bird an intruder and chase it or drive it away from the dishes. Consequently, I hang a cage containing the newcomer on the aviary wall, approximately at eye level. At night I put the bird, still in its cage, in the shelter with the other parakeets. After a few days the cage door can be opened, and the parakeet can decide for itself when it dares to venture out. If the flock reacts aggressively, the newcomer can take refuge in the cage at any time. It usually takes only a few days for the bird to become so familiar with its environment and its fellows that the cage can be removed.

Pointer: I recommend that every new bird you acquire spend about 10 days in a cage before it is integrated into a flock. During this time you can check the state of its health and have the stool examined for possible pathogenic organisms or parasites.

Bringing a Pair Together in an Aviary Compartment

If you want to breed a parakeet species and have bought a suitable mate for your bird, proceed in a similar fashion. Put a cage holding the new bird in the aviary compartment. The cage door can be opened the very next day. If at all possible, watch the two parakeets round the clock. If serious fighting breaks out, house the new arrival in a vacant neighboring compartment so that the two parakeets can spend several weeks getting acquainted through the wire mesh. If you watch carefully, you can determine whether it is a case of lifelong antipathy or merely some initial difficulties. If there is mutual dislike, the parakeets will fight each other through the wire mesh. If this happens, the newcomer will have to be exchanged, if possible, or live in another compartment farther away. If the two gradually make friends through the netting, however, you can try again after a few weeks to hang the cage with the newcomer in the aviary compartment.

Pointer: When a pair is brought together, often the male parakeet harasses the female—especially if the male had previously lived alone in the flight. In such a case you can clip the male's wings to render him temporarily unable to fly. To do so, cut the outermost three primary flight feathers on each wing. The female will be better able to escape to a safe place. If you have never clipped a parakeet's wings, have an experienced breeder or veterinarian show you how before you attempt it yourself.

Bringing a Pair Together in a Cage

If you have decided to give your hitherto solitary bird a mate, follow the same basic principle outlined above for the aviary. Put the two cages side by side so that the birds first can get acquainted through the bars. Give the new bird a few days to get used to the strange environment; then open the cage doors. If the birds make friends, soon you can put them together in one cage.

Generally, a parakeet that already has settled in will not be overjoyed to accept a new partner. At first it will defend its territory and demonstrate its superiority. To prevent serious injuries, put the new bird in a temporary cage and hang it in the aviary.

Wild budgerigars drinking and bathing. Sometimes thousands of birds gather at a watering place.

Promoting Trust

Especially at first, try to avoid unnecessary disturbances such as noisy work in the parakeets' vicinity. Try to gain the birds' confidence little by little. Patience is essential and will be rewarded!

How to Promote Trust

The following suggestions are based on my own experience and that of other knowledgeable keepers of pet parakeets. These ideas should help you win the trust of your own birds. Nothing, however, can replace your own careful observation and sensitivity. Read the section on body language in the chapter Understanding Parakeets (see page 56) and observe your birds' behavior carefully. Awareness of what your parakeets are "saying" will enable you to win their confidence more rapidly.

• Perform all chores involving the aviary or cage at the same time each day. The birds will adjust quickly to this routine.

• Never approach your birds in silence. Birds are mistrustful of silent creatures. Talk or whistle when you are in their hearing range, and talk to them while you are with them.

• Near the parakeets, play a radio at moderate volume several hours a day. This will accustom the birds to human voices.

• Avoid making hasty movements and unnecessary noise.

• In the first few weeks, avoid appearing in front of your parakeets in attention-getting clothing—for example, a large hat or dark sunglasses. It could frighten the birds.

• Once you have learned what seeds and fresh fruits and vegetables your parakeets prefer, you can try to establish closer contact by offering small "gifts."

Pointer: If you have only a single parakeet or one pair, a highly intimate relationship with the birds will develop. Then you can try to tame your parakeets or teach them individual words and short sentences. (See Useful Addresses and Literature, page 95.)

Dangers for Parakeets

However careful you are, it unfortunately is a common occurrence for parakeets to fly away or to meet with an accident while at liberty indoors.

Flying Away

A parakeet can escape when an outdoor aviary is opened, for example, or fly away through a window that has been left open. Escaped birds are in great danger, because it is hard for them to find suitable food outdoors. Moreover, rain, cold, or snow rapidly exhaust them, and they make easy victims for birds of prey. Even if a parakeet escapes in warm weather, it is not certain that the bird will find its way back. That is more likely for a bird living in an outdoor aviary, because it is acquainted with the surroundings and its mate probably will call to it. If you discover an escapee nearby in a tree or a bush, you still have a chance to get it back. First, lock all the parakeets in the night shelter. Then hang a cage holding a "decoy" right under the roof of the flight. Open the roof cover wide enough for the escaped bird to make its way easily into its familiar flight and to its fellows. If the bird is sitting in a tree at a height you can reach, you also can spray it carefully with the garden hose, so that it is temporarily unable to fly. Then the parakeet may let you catch it in your hand. Of course, a bit of luck is necessary in both cases.

The First Flight

Single birds or pairs that live in a cage or a relatively small indoor aviary need to get daily exercise by flying

When a bird is flying free indoors, the windows and doors must be closed without fail. Tame parakeets rarely will escape of their own free will, but a sudden noise or an unexpected movement can startle them and send them flying out an open window.

Dangers for Parakeets

Dangers

Open doors: The birds sit on them. When you shut a door, injuries can result.

Floors: A parakeet can be killed if it is stepped on.

Containers of water: The birds like to drink from vases and pails and may try to bathe in them; they can drown in this way.

Wastepaper baskets, ornamental vases: The bird may slip in and starve, or suffer fear-induced heart failure because it cannot get out on its own.

Flypaper: The kind that flies stick to can be death traps for birds as well.

Stove burner plates or rings: Fatal burns can result if a bird lands on a burner plate that is still hot.

Appliances and electric cords: Fatal shock can result if the bird contacts live wires.

Blazing sun: Built-up heat behind glass panes can cause heart failure.

Fluctuating temperatures: Sharp fluctuations result in colds or heatstroke.

Poisons: Fatal poisoning can be caused by detergents, household cleansers, cat litter, pencil lead, ballpoint and felt-tip pen points, room sprays, insecticidal sprays, chemically treated wood chips or shavings, medications (even cough drops), or poisonous plants (see Glossary).

How to Avoid the Danger

Before closing a door, always look to see where the bird is perched.

Always look at the floors when you walk.

Cover containers, and don't let the bird fly free when you are cleaning house.

Use woven baskets: line smooth inside surfaces with wire netting. Fill ornamental vases with sand.

Do not use flypaper.

Set a pot of cold water on a hot burner that is not in use. Never let birds fly unsupervised in the kitchen.

Place appliances and electric cords out of the bird's reach.

Provide a shady place and keep the air circulating.

Accustom birds gradually to temperature changes between 41 and 86°F (5–30°C).

Keep all these substances or objects where birds cannot reach them. Remove all traces completely. Do not put poisonous plants in the aviary or room where birds are kept.

Put screens on the windows of the room where your parakeets live; then the birds will be unable to escape. (Drawing: Cockatiel)

around in the room. Before the first free flight, you will have to eliminate all potential dangers: Close the doors and windows and draw the curtains. If you have no curtains, let down the blinds or shades to a level about 8 inches (20 cm) above the windowsill and turn on the light if need be. The bird first has to learn that windowpanes are barriers that limit its movement. Each day, leave slightly more of the windowpane uncovered, until the bird understands that the pane limits its space.

Hygiene Is Important

If you have only one pair of parakeets, you can manage with the procedures for care outlined in the plan (see page 34) that I have put together for you. However, if you have several parakeets living in a common flight or in pairs in neighboring compartments of an aviary, additional exhaustive measures are called for. You will have to disinfect the birds' quarters at regular intervals. Once a year, clean the area thoroughly and see that all necessary repairs are carried out.

Pointer: When you disinfect or do the annual large-scale cleaning, the birds have to be caught and taken out of the aviary or the aviary compartments and placed in cages for several hours. With an outdoor aviary, the birds also can be locked in the night shelter while the flight is being disinfected, and vice versa.

A thorough bath is a source of great pleasure for the Australian Pennant's parakeets.

Using Disinfectants

Particularly if several parakeets are living together in an aviary, you will have to disinfect the flight, dishes, perches, and toys at regular intervals. This helps prevent illnesses among the flock. For regular disinfection, use only mild disinfectants that present no danger for the birds. Make absolutely certain that the product does not contain formaldehyde: On a long-term basis, this highly toxic substance would impair the health of your parakeets. If you are unsure, ask your veterinarian what to use. If you need a disinfectant to destroy certain disease-causing organisms, the veterinarian also can prescribe a special product.

Commonly Used Disinfectants

Available through grocery stores, pet stores, veterinarians, and janitorial supply houses.

Lysol Manufactured by Lehn & Fials Products, Div. of Sterling Drug Inc. Dilution: 4 ounces per gallon water. All purpose disinfectant.

One-Stroke Environ Manufactured by Vestal. Dilution: ½ ounce per gallon water. All-purpose disinfectant; official disinfectant of the USDA.

Clorox Manufactured by the Clorox Co. Dilution: 6 ounces per gallon water. May be irritating to skin; may be corrosive to bare metal. Excellent for concrete flooring.

Betadine Manufactured by Purdue-Frederick, Inc. Dilution: ¾ ounce per gallon water. Excellent noncorrosive disinfectant, but more expensive. Available through veterinarians.

Note: Always follow manufacturers' recommendations.

Pointer: If you have misgivings about using disinfectants at all, you can also disinfect with a hot solution of vinegar and water or suds made with soft soap. These are less effective, however.

Good hygiene is indispensable to parakeets' well-being. The relatively small habitat to which they are confined in captivity has to be kept scrupulously clean; otherwise, dangerous disease-causing organisms will make their appearance.

Care Plan

Daily

In the morning:
- Empty all food and water dishes and bathing vessels, wash them with hot water, dry them, and refill them with fresh food and water.
- Brush the droppings off the perches, branches, cage bars, or wire netting.
- Brush or vacuum the feeding shelf or table.
- Cage bottom or indoor aviary floor: With a small shovel, remove the droppings, feathers, and leftover food.
- Outdoor aviary floor: Use a small rake to clean up the waste.

In the evening: Remove any perishable food left from the morning. Always turn off the lights at the same time, if you have no automatic dimmer switch. (See Lighting, page 22.)

There are special disinfectants that you can use to make a direct attack on pathogens such as bacteria, viruses, fungi, or parasites. If you need to control any of these organisms, ask your veterinarian to recommend the right product.

Most parakeets enjoy a lukewarm shower with a plant sprayer. They lift their wings and turn and twist so that the mist can reach everywhere. (Drawing: Cockatiel)

Pointer: If your parakeets are brooding, do only the most necessary cleaning chores, because the females are easily upset. It is enough to wash the food, water, and bathing dishes with hot water daily, dry them, and fill them again.

My tip: For cleaning, get brushes with rust-proof brass bristles and trowels of various sizes; they work well.

Weekly

- Empty and wash food dishes made of high-grade steel and simmer them for three minutes in water at a temperature of 203°F (95°C). If the dishes are made of plastic, make sure they are heat resistant; if in doubt, just rinse them in hot water.
- Remove calcium deposits from bathing and water dishes by soaking them for 30 minutes in a solution of hot water and dishwasher detergent. Finally, rinse the containers several times with fresh water, and let them dry.
- Remove the perches and branches and brush them off. Disinfect them, rinse them thoroughly, and let them dry.
- Brush or vacuum the feeding shelf or table, disinfect it, and rinse thoroughly.
- In a cage or an indoor aviary, remove the sand, disinfect the floor, wipe it clean with fresh water, and sprinkle in new sand.
- In an outdoor aviary, clean the sand floor as you do daily and add sand if necessary. If the floor is earth, do the usual daily cleaning.

Every Four to Ten Weeks
(Interim cleaning)
- Remove all containers and movable objects and clean them as directed under the weekly procedures. Put up new cuttlebones or mineral blocks.
- Remove the perch branches and

clean them as you do weekly; replace them with new ones as needed.
• Brush off or vacuum the feeding shelf, disinfect it, and rinse it off thoroughly.
• In a cage or an indoor aviary, remove the sand on the floor, vacuum the floor, disinfect it, wash it thoroughly with fresh water, and sprinkle on new sand.
• In an outdoor aviary, clean the sand floor as you do daily and add sand if necessary. Clean an earth floor as you do daily.
• Disinfect aviary or cage frames, wire mesh, windows, heaters, and doors. Rinse them well and rub them dry.
• Corners, cracks, guide slots, and branch mounts should be brushed out or brushed off, vacuumed, disinfected, wiped thoroughly clean, and allowed to dry.

Once a Year
(Major renovation)

If several parakeets live in your aviary, it is preferable to renovate it thoroughly in the spring.
• First, proceed exactly as for the interim cleaning (see above).
• Vacuum or brush off the nest boxes, disinfect them inside and out, rinse them thoroughly, and let them air-dry. Return the disinfected nest boxes to their customary places.
• The ceilings, walls, doors, and window frames should be brushed off and washed, disinfected, wiped thoroughly clean, and allowed to dry. Smooth out any uneven, rough, or porous places on the walls and plaster them if necessary. Apply fresh paint and ventilate well before you let the birds return to their enclosure.
• Carry out all necessary repairs and maintenance.
• Concrete aviary floor: Remove the soil or sand filler and replace it with new material; set new plants as needed. (See page 22.)

If you can set up a "shower corner" for your parakeets, don't deny them this special treat. (Drawing: Left: Nanday parakeet; right: Red-rumped parakeet)

• Nonconcrete aviary floor: Remove the topsoil three or four times a year and replace it with fresh soil. Alternatively, burn off the surface of the topsoil, using a Bunsen burner, and remove and replace the soil only every two years; set new plants if necessary. (See page 22.)

Important: After every large-scale cleaning and interim cleaning, disinfect your tools and vacuum cleaner!

Proper Nutrition

Parakeets live chiefly on seeds, but occasionally they also enjoy eating fresh fruits, vegetables, and wild plants. A varied diet will keep your charges healthy and happy.

What Parakeets Like

Parakeets living in the wild have available a great variety of highly nutritious foods. Everything they eat is newly ripened and thus offers maximum nutritional value. Their diet includes seeds, buds, young leaves, fruits, berries, flower nectar, and pollen. In addition, they peel off the bark of twigs and pick tiny stones out of the ground, which aid their digestive processes. Some scientists suspect that parakeets even eat insect larvae, tiny insects, and aquatic snails and get the protein they require in this way. Consequently, it is not so easy to find substitutes for the range of foods available in nature. With some effort and consideration, however, it is possible to provide captive parakeets with a highly nutritious diet, so that you can enjoy healthy birds with shiny feathers for many years to come.

Seeds as a Staple

Most likely, a pet store dealer or breeder has given you information about your parakeets' basic diet until now. If you keep various species, you may possibly have to offer them different seed mixes, depending on each parakeet's body size and the strength of its bill. Ready-to-use mixes are available commercially, as well as individually packaged varieties of seeds.

The first few times you refill the dishes with the seed mix, check to see which types of seeds the birds have picked out as their favorites. Then you can put together your own mixtures or offer the birds their special favorites in extra dishes. You will also avoid a great deal of waste in this way.

Seed mixes should contain the following:

For large parakeets, such as the mallee ringneck, superb parakeet, and regent parakeet: various types of millets, polished seeds, oats, wheat, pumpkin seed, sunflower seed (white, striped, and black), and—for cold days—some hemp and niger seed.

For small species, such as the turquoise parakeet, Bourke's parakeet, and budgerigar: 75 percent of the total amount of seeds consists of various varieties of millets. The remainder is made up of polished seeds, small sunflower seeds, canary grass seeds, wheat, oats, linseed, and—for cold days—a little hemp seed, niger, and poppy seed. Small parakeets in particular should not be deprived of their beloved spray millet. Large parakeets also enjoy it.

My tip: Fatty seeds like sunflower seed should make up about 8 percent of the mixture. During the brooding period, this share should be increased to 20 percent. Sunflower seed and pumpkin seed should be offered unshelled to the birds, because they enjoy using their bills to remove the husks.

In their native habitat, the South American Quaker parakeets can cause great damage in corn fields. For this reason, ruthless measures often are taken to combat them.

HOW-TO
Fresh Food

1|Place soaked seeds in the sprouting dishes.

A varied diet will keep your parakeets healthy. For this reason, they must have fresh foods such as sprouts, vegetables, and fruits in addition to their daily mix of bird seeds.

Vitamin Enrichment: Sprouted Grains

Approximately every six weeks, you can enrich the daily offerings of fresh foods by providing sprouted seeds. If the birds are given them for about 20 days, additional vitamin supplements (see Vitamins and Minerals, page 42) usually are unnecessary. During the entire incubation period and the raising of the young, sprouted seeds should be part of the daily menu.

All the seeds listed in the section on staple foods are suitable for sprouting. To ensure that the seeds will sprout, I rec-ommend that you buy a sprout "silo," available in pet stores.

Pointer: It is essential to check on the nutritional value of all seeds before you use them, by making a germination test (see page 40).

Sprouting Seeds with the Sprout "Silo"

A sprout silo consists of three, four, or more round sprouting dishes with small siphon caps and a water collecting dish. Before the seeds are put in the silo, they have to soak. Put them in a glass dish, cover them with water, and let them soak there for 24 hours, loosely covered. You will need about 2 tablespoons of mixed seeds for each parakeet every day.

2|Every day, pour ½ pint (¼ L) of water in the top dish.

Drawing 1
After the seeds have soaked, put them in a fine-meshed sieve and rinse them in lukewarm water. Put them in the sprouting dishes, leaving the bottom dish (water collecting dish) empty.

Drawing 2
Stack all the dishes on top of one another and carefully pour ½ pint (¼ L) of water in the top dish. The water will automatically run via the tiny siphon tubes through the individual dishes, cover the seeds, then collect in the drip dish at the bottom.
Put the silo in a bright place, but not in direct sun, and pour water in once a day as directed above.

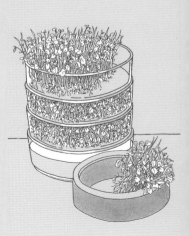

3|Remove the sprouts in portions and serve them to the birds.

Drawing 3
Once sprouts are shooting forth from the seeds or little stems are rising up, they are ready to be fed to the parakeets. First, put the sprouts in a sieve, rinse them with lukewarm water, and let them drip dry. Serve them in a dish by themselves.

My tip: Nesting dishes for canaries (available in pet stores) make good dishes for serving sprouts. Made of plastic, the dishes have small holes that will let air circulate through the sprouts, thus retarding spoilage. In any case, remove any uneaten sprouts after half a day at most.

Serving Fresh Foods Properly
Fruits, vegetables, and herbs are essential components of your parakeets' daily diet. I explain on page 41 which fresh foods you can give your birds and which are unsuitable for them. It is important to serve fruits, vegetables, and herbs to the parakeets in such a way that they can eat them easily and with enjoyment. Drawings 4 and 5 show useful examples. Hard fruits and vegetables—a slice of apple or a carrot, for example—can be wedged between the bars. You can also grate them coarsely, mix them with lettuce cut into small pieces, leafy vegetables, and cubes of fruits. Serve this mixture in a dish as shallow as possible.

My tip: Parakeets especially like to nibble on fresh ears of corn and fresh spray millet with half-ripened seeds (organically grown). You can freeze both to have a supply for the winter.

Drawing 4
Parakeets can eat hard fruits like apples, pears, or carrots only if you spear fairly large

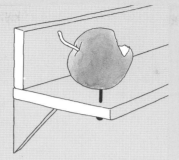

4|Spear apples and carrots on a dull nail.

chunks securely on a blunt nail protruding from the feeding shelf, so that the birds can chew on them there.

Drawing 5
Make bunches of herbs, wild plants, and ears of grain and hang them on a branch. These foods can be fastened to the aviary mesh with a clothespin or undyed strips of raffia.

Soft Fresh Foods
For large parakeets—the regent parakeet, superb parakeet, and mallee ringneck, for example— cut soft fruits and vegetables such as bananas and eggplants

into 1- to 1½-inch (3–4 cm) pieces and serve them in a dish as wide and shallow as possible—an earthenware saucer, for example. For smaller species—budgerigars or Bourke's parakeets—cut the foods into smaller cubes.

My tip: Don't be discouraged if your parakeets are timid about sampling the fresh foods. Make the offerings as varied as possible: Parakeets are curious. You can, for example, attach halved, seeded green peppers to favorite branch perches with a piece of twine, so that the birds can reach them easily (see Drawing 5). At first, sheer curiosity will lead them to take a nibble, then they will begin to enjoy the taste, and soon the pepper will rank as a delicacy.

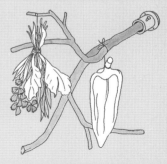

5|Parakeets greatly enjoy pecking at food tied to a branch.

39

Sprouting Test

Do not store seeds too long, because vitamins and other nutritive substances break down during storage. Before you give seeds to your birds, conduct a germination test to check their nutritional value:

• Put one teaspoonful of seeds into a glass dish and cover with ¾ inch (2 cm) of water. Cover the dish loosely, so that air can still get in.

• Let the seeds soak for 24 hours, then transfer them to a sieve, rinse under lukewarm water, and let them drip dry.

• Put the seeds back into the glass dish, cover them loosely, and put them in a bright place at room temperature to germinate for 48 hours.

If roughly 60 percent of the seeds sprout, the quality is good.

Signs of Spoilage

• Decay: Rotten seeds smell musty; good ones are odorless.

• Rancid seed: Can be identified by its taste. (Sample the seed.)

• Mold: The seeds have a whitish coating. Examine them very carefully! Mold leads to fatal illnesses. (See Aspergillosis in Glossary.)

• Insects: The seeds stick together in clumps, with filaments as thin as cobwebs visible among them.

• Poisonous ergot: Examine all seeds of grain for the presence of ergot (see Glossary). Ergot is blackish in color

Even the tiniest puddle can support life—yellow-vented blue bonnet (Psephotus haematogaster) in Australia.

and noticeably larger than the other seeds.

• Contaminated seeds: Unclean seeds and oil seeds contain disease-causing organisms. Broken seeds are of poor quality.

Store them properly: Store all seeds in a dark, well-ventilated, dry place where they cannot be reached by pests and rodents. Small linen bags or a feed box made of wood are best for this purpose.

Wild Plants to Gather
Seeds, flowers, and leaves are foods of high nutritional value, and the process of eating them keeps parakeets occupied as well.

Grass seeds: Low spear grass (*Poa annua*), Kentucky bluegrass (*Poa pratensis*), English rye grass (*Lolium perenne*), and velvet grass (*Holcus lanatus*).

Flowers and seeds: Chickweed (*Stellaria media*), sorrel (*Rumex acetosa*), shepherd's purse (*Capsella bursa-pastoris*), and dandelion (*Taraxacum officinale*), after flowering is past, when the tips of the placentas (spermatophores) are just barely visible.

Varieties of millet and knotgrass: Barnyard grass (*Panicum crus-galli*), finger grass or crab grass (*Panicum sanguinale*), green foxtail (*Setaria viridis*), true millet (*Panicum miliaceum*), sow thistle (*Sonchus oleraceus*), common knotweed (*Polygonum aviculare*), and lady's thumb (*Polygonum persicaria*).

Berries and fruits: Wild chicory (*Cichorium intybus*), rowan berries, pyracantha berries, rose hips.

Caution: Gather only the wild plants that you recognize. To learn more, study specialized books. (See Useful Addresses and Literature, page 95.) Do not gather wild plants along the edges of roads and fields. They are poisoned by car exhaust fumes,

fertilizers, and pesticides. Before you feed any wild plants to a bird, wash them well in lukewarm water and shake them dry.

My tip: Freeze berries, fruits, and seeds of wild plants in appropriate portions for use during the winter months. Grow chickweed and other herbs year-round in little boxes or flower pots.

Fruits and Vegetables
Daily servings of fruits and vegetables are just as essential for your parakeets as the staple foods.

Raw vegetables: Eggplant, chicory, green peas and pea pods, pieces of ears of corn or half-ripe kernels cut off the cob, spinach leaves, small pieces of iceberg lettuce, escarole, carrots, zucchini, mild onions, tomatoes, celery stalks, fennel bulbs, green peppers, and watercress.

These are indigestible: All kinds of cabbage, raw potatoes, green potatoes, leaf lettuce that has been chemically sprayed, and avocados.

Fruit: Pineapple, apricots, peeled apples, bananas (unpeeled and cut in slices about 1½ inches [4 cm] thick), peeled pears, blackberries, strawberries, raspberries, currants, grapes, fresh dates and figs, cherries, peeled kiwi fruit, peeled cactus figs, peeled mangoes, tangerines, oranges, melons, peaches, papayas, and persimmons.

These are indigestible: Grapefruits, lemons, plums, rhubarb, and all dried fruits, that are treated with sulfur dioxide. (There are, however, mixtures of dried fruit and nuts or seeds that are especially prepared for cage and aviary birds.)

In a water dispenser, drinking water will stay clean, because dirt can scarcely get into the tiny drinking dish. When you buy a dispenser, look for one that has a mount for horizontal cage bars.

Vitamins and Minerals

If you feed your parakeets a varied diet that includes plenty of fresh fruits and vegetables, they are unlikely to suffer from vitamin and mineral deficiencies. Their requirements increase, however, when they are molting, laying and brooding, raising their young, getting used to a new environment, grieving over the loss of a mate, or in need of more sunlight. During these times, your parakeets need a multivitamin supplement containing Vitamins A, B, C, and E. You can sprinkle it in powdered form on their proteins (see right). In addition, cuttlebones or mineral blocks for sharpening bills should be available at all times. They help a parakeet keep its beak in shape and also provide necessary elements. Look for this information on the package: "Limestone contains everything necessary for building the skeleton and forming the feathers." Bird sand and bird gravel also contain important minerals. If the aviary floor is covered with soil, provide bird sand in a dish. In addition, always supply the birds with a calcium preparation that contains sodium carbonate, phosphorus, manganese, magnesium, iodine, iron, copper, cobalt, and potash. All the products mentioned are available in pet stores.

Although parakeets by their nature drink little, they need their daily water ration. Supply fresh, clean water every day. Noncarbonated mineral water is even better.

Many parakeets use one foot to hold their food. (Drawing: Cockatiel)

Important: Pay attention to the date indicating the shelf life of the vitamins.

Protein

Particularly when parakeets are incubating and raising their young, they need food high in protein to raise healthy, vigorous offspring. About two months before the brooding season, start feeding your parakeets protein, so that they can get used to it gradually. It does all birds good to get about one tablespoon of protein once or twice a week. Pet stores sell a ready-to-use form of protein. A mixture of "Universal Plus" and CeDeMix in a 2:1 ratio has proved reliable. You can easily prepare animal protein yourself, however.

Here's how: Finely chop hard-boiled egg yolk. Soften some stale white bread—without any trace of mold—in water, squeeze out the moisture, and mix the bread with an equal amount of egg yolk. Alternatively, mix the yolk with a small amount of low-fat farmer's cheese and finely crushed zwieback in a 2:1:1 ratio. (If the resulting paste is too thick, thin it with some carrot juice from a health food store.)

Especially when your birds are raising young, regularly supplement commercial and home-prepared forms of protein with fruit, wild plants, and sprouted seeds (see How-To, page 38). This is the only way for the parents to give their young food with a high nutritional value.

The right amount: While your parakeets are raising their young, give large birds about one tablespoonful of protein daily; small birds need about one teaspoonful.

Pointer: Protein spoils quickly, so remove any leftovers after about two hours.

Drinking Water

Parakeets need fresh, clean drinking water daily. In an outdoor aviary, put the water containers in the covered part of the flight. Automatic water dispensers will keep the water from getting dirty quickly. Never put water dishes next to food, because the birds also try to bathe in their drinking water, and the seeds would get wet.

The ideal drinking water supply for summer would be running water that flows from a miniature fountain. The birds would always have fresh water to drink, and they could bathe in the shallow collecting basin.

Important Rules for Feeding

• Every morning after your maintenance chores, give the parakeets fresh supplies (seeds, fresh fruits and vegetables, water for bathing and drinking).
• Remove the fresh fruits and vegetables at about noon, because they spoil quickly.
• The amount of food is determined by the size and number of the birds.

Rule of thumb: For birds with a body length up to 10 inches (25 cm), allow about two tablespoons of seeds and half a cup of fresh fruits and vegetables per bird; for larger parakeets, four tablespoons of seeds and one cup of fruits and vegetables per bird. Do not underfeed the birds. As time goes on, you will learn what their actual requirements are.

Pointer: Seeds left untouched in the dish need not be thrown away if they are not dirty. Discard the empty hulls and pour the uneaten seeds, together with new ones, into a clean food dish.

My tip: If your parakeets live in an outdoor aviary with a night shelter, I recommend that all the seeds be given to them in the shelter, where they will not get wet. In addition, the waste from seeds is easier to clean up in the shelter than in the flight.

Feed the birds their sprouts, fruits, and vegetables in the flight.

Like members of their species that live in the wild, cage and aviary parakeets also like to pick up grain from the ground. (Drawing: Scarlet-chested parakeets)

If Parakeets Get Sick

Good care, impeccable hygiene, and a balanced diet help you prevent many of the diseases that affect parakeets. Overcrowded enclosures and quarreling inhabitants create stress and make the birds vulnerable to disease.

Even with impeccable care and loving attention, your parakeets may get sick. If you keep your birds in an aviary, there is a danger that the birds will infect each other. For this reason it is important to observe your parakeets closely several times a day. If you know your birds well, you will notice immediately if one of them shows any change in behavior. A change in the droppings, malformed feathers, or untouched food dishes also point to the existence of a health problem.

Pointer: If your birds live in an outdoor aviary, it is advisable to have a stool sample tested once a year. Additionally, in spring and fall, arrange with your veterinarian for the birds to be given preventive treatments for roundworms (*Ascaris*) and threadworms (*Capillaria*).

Stressful Situations

Stress makes parakeets more susceptible to disease. Many stressful situations, however, can be prevented or alleviated. Negative conditions such as an unbalanced or poor diet and crowded enclosures, for example, can be avoided. Brooding and raising young are naturally occurring sources of stress for birds, but you still can make these situations easier for them. The best solution is to isolate the brooding pairs in a sufficiently large aviary compartment, free of disturbances. If competitive struggles break out between independent young birds and their parents, it is time to move the young parakeets into their own quarters.

How to Tell a Sick Parakeet

Parakeets that are indisposed or ill usually are apathetic. They sit for hours in one place, with their plumage slightly ruffled and their bill stuck into their back feathers, and often rest on both legs. This listlessness is often accompanied by loss of appetite and drowsiness, and sometimes the bird also will let its wings or tail droop and sit with its body held almost horizontally, rather than upright, on a branch. If a parakeet behaves in this way, put a piece of paper under its resting place, so that you can examine the consistency of the droppings and have them tested if necessary. In addition, isolate the bird in a hospital cage (see What to Do First, page 46) to protect the other inhabitants of the aviary from the possibility of an infectious disease.

Other Signs of Illness:

- Continually watery droppings, light green or gray in color; droppings that are foamy or mixed with blood. (Obtain a stool sample and have it tested by a veterinarian.)
- Nasal discharge.
- Slimy substances secreted from the mouth or cloaca.
- Labored breathing, possibly also noisy.
- The bird waggles its tail when it breathes.
- Fits of trembling, cramps, or even paralysis.
- Bleeding from a wound or from the cloaca.

The ringneck parakeet has the largest geographic range of any parrot. It is equally at home in Africa and India. In Africa, the subspecies *P. k. krameri* (African ringneck parakeet) is quite common. In India, the subspecies *P. k. manillensis* (Indian ringneck parakeet) ranks as the most common parrot of all.

Natural branches of varied diameter let parakeets exercise their feet and keep them healthy.

- Continually ruffled feathers. (Immediately after flying, the feathers normally remain ruffled for a short time.)
- Constant fussing with the feathers.
- Overgrown beak and claws.

Important: All these symptoms are to be taken seriously. The bird must be brought to a veterinarian without delay.

What to Do First

Once the parakeet has been isolated as a precautionary measure, it needs peace, quiet, and steady warmth. A hospital cage, available in pet stores, is best, because the heat is thermostatically controlled. You can, however, also place an infrared lamp next to an ordinary cage at a distance of about 12 inches (30 cm). Arrange it so that the bird can choose to sit within or outside the heated area. Because humid air is helpful in easing the symptoms of many diseases, set a bowl of hot water between the heat source and the cage; this will increase the atmospheric humidity. If the bird's illness is not serious, this heat treatment alone may bring relief. You can leave the lamp on for 48 hours and more. The temperature in the cage area should be 84 to 86°F (29–30°C). If your parakeet shows improvement, before you turn off the lamp, gradually increase the distance between it and the cage. This will allow the temperature to drop slowly. It will take several hours! An abrupt drop in temperature could result in a cold or cause a relapse. If no improvement is evident after 24 hours, see a veterinarian.

Caution: If your bird has cramps, the heat treatment can be harmful. In this case, consult a veterinarian at once.

The right way to cut overgrown claws: Do not injure the blood vessels, which are faintly visible inside the horny substance of the nail. Hold the claw in front of a lamp to see the blood vessels better. Don't blunt the claw when you trim it; it should be pointed.

Going to the Veterinarian

Not all veterinarians are familiar with the diseases that befall parrots and parakeets. The Association of Avian Veterinarians (see page 95) can provide you with addresses of veterinarians with relevant experience.

In addition, some universities have institutes of avian diseases, which generally also employ avian specialists.

A sick parakeet has to be protected from heat, cold, and damp and brought to the veterinarian via the shortest route possible. If you have no car, take a pet taxi, now available in some cities.

My tip: Find out the address of an experienced avian veterinarian well ahead of time, so that you do not lose valuable time looking for one when a bird falls ill.

Don't Forget:

- Take a stool sample with you to the veterinarian.
- Have the veterinarian explain every necessary procedure in detail and demonstrate it to you. Instructions in writing help you remember.
- Give the bird its prescribed medications exactly as the veterinarian directed, and continue the medications for the recommended length of time. If necessary, have the doctor show you how to administer medication to the bird.
- In many cities, an avian veterinarian is available on call for emergencies at night and on holidays. Doctors on duty for emergencies are usually listed in the membership newsletters of bird societies and clubs.

Psittacosis

Psittacosis, also known as ornithosis, chlamydiosis, or parrot fever, is a highly contagious disease that affects not only parrots, as previously believed, but also songbirds, pigeons, and domestic fowl. The following symptoms appear singly or together: apathy, drowsiness, loss of appetite, watery feces, head cold, shortness of breath, conjunctivitis with a discharge of pus from the lower eyelids, fits of trembling.

If such symptoms are evident in a bird, it has to be isolated immediately and treated with heat. (See What to Do First, page 46.) The bird's chance of recovery is best if it is brought to a veterinarian within 24 hours.

In the meantime, you can have the droppings of healthy parakeets tested for the presence of the organisms that cause psittacosis, or ornithosis. Parakeets may carry the disease without showing any signs of illness and without catching the disease themselves.

Psittacosis also can be transmitted to humans. It can be dangerous, particularly for the elderly and for people with circulatory problems. The disease manifests itself as flu or as a mild case of pneumonia, and it is curable if detected and treated promptly.

An outbreak of psittacosis must be reported to the authorities. The veterinarian will tell you what to do if the need arises.

Feather Plucking
This phenomenon, which is unrelated to the annual molt (see Molt in Glossary), has not been studied sufficiently to classify it with certainty as a mental disorder or as a deficiency disease. Parrots and parakeets that are kept singly are the predominant sufferers. They often start plucking out their feathers quite suddenly. In many cases, only the head area is left with its feathers. If your parakeet behaves in this way, I suggest that you consult a veterinarian. Many ornithologists attribute feather plucking to psychological disorders caused by the loss of a significant human or a mate, a change of environment, or the lack of a mate

at the onset of puberty. Other scientists cite crowded enclosures, lack of exercise, poor diet, lack of bathing facilities, or parasites.

Feather Malformations
In older, malnourished, or not entirely healthy parakeets, malformed feathers may appear after the molt (see Glossary). The possible causes are dietary deficiencies, hormonal disturbances, or cysts in the feather follicles. The bird must be examined and treated by a veterinarian.

Using an infrared lamp to give your sick parakeet a heat treatment is the first step you can take to help the bird.

47

If Parakeets Are Going to Brood

B reeding para-
keets generally
aims to keep a spe-
cies pure-bred and
healthy. Selection
based on plumage
colors and body
shapes is practiced,
for example, in the
breeding of budgeri-
gars and cockatiels.

If you want your parakeets to have
offspring, you will have to make some
preparations in advance. If you keep
different parakeet species, you will
have to provide each breeding pair
with its own compartment in the outdoor aviary and in the night shelter or
with separate indoor aviaries, because
many parakeet parents become aggressive when they brood. In a community aviary, where particularly
peaceable species of parakeets live
together, you do not need separate
compartments. On page 29, I have
described procedures for getting parakeets of different sexes used to one
another.

Pointer: In the table on page 88,
you will find important information on
breeding all the parakeet species discussed in this book, including the
length of the incubation period, the
size of the nesting box, and the size
of the leg band.

Moving into the Nest Box
First offer two different nest boxes
(see How-To, page 54) to every pair
of parakeets that you intend to breed,
so that the birds can choose between
them. If your birds live in an outdoor
aviary, spring is the best time for
brooding. If the parakeets are housed
in an indoor aviary, you can offer
them nest boxes at any time of year.
The female first will inspect the nest
boxes and make her choice clear by
staying longer in one of the boxes.
Then you can remove the other box.
With increasing frequency, you now
will see the male striving to impress
the female through his behavior. Not

long thereafter, courtship begins, and
one day mating will occur (see page
58).

As soon as the parakeets are
brooding, enter the aviary only in the
mornings for feeding and cleaning,
because during the initial days of incubation the female is very easily
upset by disturbances and might stop
sitting on the eggs. The temperature
in the nesting area (a room indoors or
the aviary night shelter) should range
between 55 and 64°F (13–18°C) (see
Brooding Temperature in Glossary).

Pointer: If you want your parakeets
to brood every year, offer them the
same nesting box they used the previous year, in the same location.

Laying and Brooding
Most female parakeets lay one egg
every two days and start to brood
once the second egg has been laid. It
takes about 20 days for the young to
hatch (see table, page 88).

Caution: If the female sits on the
ground with her feathers ruffled shortly
before laying, she may be egg-bound.
Catch her very carefully in a bird net
and place her in a hospital cage at a
temperature of about 86°F (30°C). If
need be, you also can put her in a
cage heated with infrared light (see
What to Do First, page 46). The temperature of the cage's surroundings
should be approximately 91°F (33°C).
The heat treatment usually causes the
cramp to relax, and the female is able
to lay the egg. If it is not laid within 12
to 24 hours, the bird—kept at the
same temperature, if possible—has to
be taken to the veterinarian. It would

be preferable for the veterinarian to come to you in this case, because the female is in grave danger.

Brooding: During incubation, the female spends the bulk of her time sitting on the clutch of eggs, and she is fed by the male (see drawing, page 63). In many species, the male feeds his mate through the next box entry hole; in others, the female flies to the male and takes the food from him outside the nesting box.

Keep your curiosity under control and do not look into the nest box during the first four days of the brooding period, lest you disturb the female.

On the fifth or sixth day, you can check (see drawing, page 50) to see whether all the eggs are fertile. Do not remove the infertile ones, however. The female would only be confused and might stop sitting.

Pointer: Do not wipe off dirty eggs; it might damage the embryos. A natural waxy layer on the eggs safeguards the embryos against infection.

When the Young Hatch

The closer the hatching date comes, the more crucial it is that the atmospheric humidity level in the nest box remain at about 80 percent (See How-To, page 54.) The process of hatching is extremely hard work for the young bird, and success is possible only if its fine skin does not get stuck inside the egg. This can easily happen if the skin is too dry. Humid air will help prevent it from drying out. Many females cover their feathers with water shortly before the eggs hatch and continue to sit on them with their feathers damp.

The Hatching Process

The young hatch in the order in which the eggs were laid. Once a chick has reached a certain stage of development, it leaves the egg. To do so, it scratches on the eggshell with its egg

A pair of turquoise parakeets.

tooth (see Glossary). Then it turns a few millimeters and pecks on the shell again, opening a crack in the thin wall of the egg. By repeated stretching movements, it finally breaks off a piece of the shell. Then it kicks until it has made its way out. The female eats the tiny pieces of eggshell to satisfy her need for calcium. Depending on the parakeet species, a newly hatched chick is more or less naked.

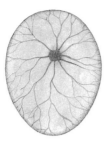

Starting on the fifth or sixth day after the eggs are laid, you can check to see whether they are fertile. Hold the eggs against the light of a powerful flashlight. In fertile eggs, a germ cell is visible, with delicate tiny blood vessels branching out from it. Eggs that are not viable are more translucent.

Some have a few downy feathers. The female has to take the hatchling under her wing (see Taking the Chicks under Her Wing in Glossary) constantly to warm it.

Pointer: As soon as the young are hatched, the parent birds will need larger amounts of protein (see page 42). They should continue to receive seeds, with the exclusion of oats and hemp, because these might too soon put the males in the mood for courtship again.

The Development of the Nestlings

The developmental phases of the nestlings vary in length, depending on the species. Nestlings of large parakeet species develop somewhat more slowly than those of smaller species. It takes four to five weeks for the young birds to become independent.

• During the first few days of life, the young are fed only by their mother, who prepares in her crop (See Glossary) the mixture most easily digestible for each nestling, depending on its age.

• Between the fifth and the seventh day, the young bird's egg tooth falls out, its eyes gradually begin to open, and the first feather quills sprout.

• Seven to ten days after hatching, the mother bird will spend more time outside the nest box.

• After about the tenth day, the nestlings may make various noises, and many will hiss if there is danger.

• After roughly 14 days, the eyes are completely open, the first downy feathers are being replaced by new ones, and the large feathers are starting to grow.

• After about 16 days, the nestlings can toddle a little.

• With many species, the father bird now starts to participate in feeding the young.

• After four to five weeks, the young

birds fly out of the nest box in the order in which they hatched.

• Several days later, they begin to feed themselves. Have soft baby bird food (see page 51) and hulled seeds ready for them.

• About three weeks after leaving the nest, the young birds finally are able to remove the husks of seeds independently.

Important: Between the tenth and the twelfth day of life, put a leg band on each nestling (see How-To, page 55).

The Daily Nest Check

After the first young birds have hatched, check the nest daily, preferably at a time when the female is outside the nest box.

• In the first few days, look to see whether any of the hatchlings has died. A dead nestling has to be removed at once; otherwise, its rapid decay will endanger its nest siblings.

• If a large amount of droppings has collected in the nest, take the young out and put them in a dish lined with soft, slightly warmed paper towels or a terry cloth towel. Put in new nesting material quickly, then return the little birds to the nest.

• You can assume that the female is giving the nestlings enough food during the first few days. Later, carefully feel the young birds to see whether their crops are full and they are developing properly.

Pointer: If the nestlings are not continuing to grow, if their crops often are only slightly filled, and if their begging noises increase, they are not getting enough to eat. Give the nestlings extra food three to four times a day, and watch closely to see whether the parents continue to feed them. If not, you will have to assume the responsibility of raising them yourself.

Hand-raising the Young

If you take over the duties of raising the nestlings, first build them a substitute nest. A plastic dish lined with soft paper towels makes the best receptacle for the young. Cover the dish with a cloth and put it in a warm place (about 98.6°F [37°C]), for example, near a radiator. If you are only giving them extra food, it is sufficient to place the young birds on a warmed terry cloth towel for their feeding. Then return them to their nest box.

Food for Hand-raising Nestlings

Twice a day, prepare a fresh supply of the formula you use for hand-feeding the baby birds and put it in the refrigerator. Ready-made mixes are commercially available in pet stores.

Feeding times: Until the eighth day of life, every two hours; thereafter every three hours, round the clock. After the fourteenth day, every four hours from 6 A.M. to 11 P.M.

The right amount: You can tell by feeling a nestling's crop whether you have given it enough to eat. The crop should be full, but not full to bursting.

Rule of thumb: If you are feeding the birds at two-hour intervals, give each nestling one tablespoonful; at three-hour intervals, two tablespoonfuls; at four-hour intervals, as much as the little bird will eat.

How to feed: Warm the food for the nestlings to their body temperature before use, preferably in a baby bottle warmer. With a small spoon, drip the food into the nestling's beak. If the baby birds have just hatched, it is preferable to use a food syringe (available in pet stores). Cover the syringe with a small piece of rubber tubing, also available in pet stores, so that the young birds do not injure themselves as they eat. After feeding the birds, clean them carefully with soft paper to remove all traces of food. Rinse the utensils in hot water.

Pointer: Weigh the young birds once a day, record their weight, and compare it with the figures for the previous day. If a nestling is not gaining weight, it is not getting enough to eat. Increase the portions.

My tip: For a beginner, feeding nestlings is not easy. Have an experienced breeder show you how to do it.

Helping Young Birds Fly

Once the young birds come up to the hole of the nest box to be fed, the time to leave the nest is not far away. They are still timid and easily frightened in their new surroundings, however, and first have to become familiar with the limits of the available flying space. To keep them from getting hurt in their first attempts to fly, take the following precautionary measures:

During mating, the male often places both wings around the female. In this state of excitement, the birds' pupils become smaller and are visible as tiny dots in the light iris. (Drawing: Budgerigars)

A female budgerigar in a brooding hollow. During the first few days of life, the nestlings li[e]

Spoon feeding young chicks. Hand feeding also is done with a syringe.

- Cover the aviary walls with reed mats. They will cushion the impact, and the young birds can cling to them.
- Attach some additional twigs and branches in the aviary for the young birds to land on.

Pointers: If one of the young has crashed into a wall and is lying or sitting on the ground, leave it alone. If it is not seriously injured, it will recover and fly or climb up after some time has passed. If it is lying in the blazing sun, attach a shield to the outside of the aviary to provide shade. Don't touch the bird; the shock could kill it. If it does not recover on its own, you will have to take it to a veterinarian.

on their backs while being fed.　　*Soon they stretch up toward their mother.*

Family Life

The young birds will stay with their parents for a few more weeks, fed mostly by their father, until they are independent. Then the parents often treat their offspring ungraciously, because they want to devote themselves to the next brood without further disturbance. If the father chases his newly fledged offspring, the young will have to move into a separate enclosure.

Important: After the second brood in a year, remove the nest boxes and do not offer them to the birds again until the following spring.

It is advisable to weigh each hand-reared chick once a day.

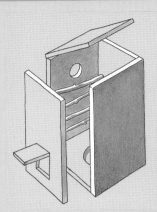

1 Upright nest box with an inspection door.

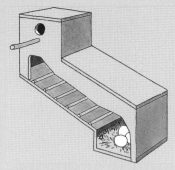

2 Sloping box with a slanting descent leading to the clutch.

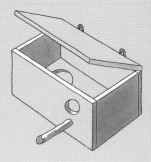

4 An oblong nest box needs no inspection door.

Pet stores offer an enormous variety of nest boxes for parakeets, but you also can build boxes yourself.

Guidelines for All Nest Boxes

Material: Only chemically untreated, unplaned natural wood. No particle board or tropical woods!

Nest box size and diameter of the entry hole (see table, page 88).

The nest cavity should have a diameter of 3½ to 4½ inches (9–11 cm) for large parakeets (with a body over 14 inches [36 cm] long); 2⅓ to 3 inches (6–8 cm) for medium-sized birds (body length 12 to 14 inches [30–35 cm]), and 2 to 2⅓ inches (5–6 cm) for all smaller birds.

Nesting material: Fill the nest cavity to a depth of about

2 inches (5 cm) with nesting material (hamster litter made of untreated wood shavings; no sawdust!).

Approach branch: It goes in front of the entry hole (2⅓ to 3 inches [6–8 cm] long).

Atmospheric humidity: Shortly before the chicks hatch, the humidity level should be about 80 percent. Use humidifiers or spray the nest box with an atomizer for plants.

A place to gnaw: Attach one or two fairly small boards of soft wood in the box.

3 A natural tree trunk is the closest thing to a brooding hollow.

The right place: Hang the box high enough for you to see inside comfortably.

Important: If the female is not vigilant about taking the chicks under her wing for warmth, attach a nest box heater (available in pet stores).

Styles of Nest Boxes
When building the nest boxes, keep the following in mind:

Upright Nest Box
Drawing 1
You must be able to fasten the inspection door in the lower third from the outside and to secure the door in open position. In addition, the door opening should be large enough for you to reach in with your hand. Inside, beneath the entry hole, attach wood strips as steps for the birds to descend.

Sloping Box
Drawing 2
This is readily accepted by parakeets, because it imitates the way into a deep hollow in a tree. The steep drop usually prevents the birds from hopping onto the clutch of eggs.

Natural Tree Trunk
Drawing 3
Many parakeets will breed only in natural trunks because of the instinct for nesting in holes in trees. Natural tree trunks are harder to clean, however.

Oblong Nest Box
Drawing 4
The nest cavity has to be located on the side opposite the entry hole, so that the female does not hop onto the clutch of eggs when she enters the box.

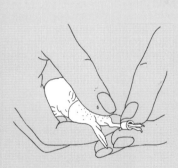

5|*When banding the leg, hold the nestling gently in the palm of your hand.*

The Leg Band
Every nestling has to be given a leg band made of metal, with a number stamped on it (see page 25). There are slightly open and completely closed leg bands, with a legally prescribed diameter (see table, page 88) that depends on the species of the parakeet. Closed bands are obtainable from your bird association.

Pointer: The leg band may be removed only if it is injuring the bird. Many parakeets get the leg band caught on a twig, tug on the band, and seriously injure their foot. Look at your birds' leg bands daily, so that any pathological changes will be noticed promptly. If necessary, have the veterinarian remove the band and give you a written statement that he has done so. Keep the band in a safe place as additional documentation.

Banding a Nestling
Between the sixth and ninth days of life, the young birds have to have their leg bands attached. I recommend that you use completely closed bands. Birds that wear them can be sold or exchanged more easily.

Drawing 5
Carefully remove the nestling from the nest box and put it in the palm of your hand. Hold the little leg gently between your thumb and forefinger.

Drawing 6
First, pull the leg band over the two front toes and the longer back toe. Then push it up slowly over the shorter back toe.

My tip: For the time being, band only one of the young birds from a brood and see whether the mother and father parakeets accept the leg band. Many parents are upset by the presence of this alien object on their nestlings and try to get it off. On more than one occasion, the parents have bitten off the young bird's entire foot. If necessary, you will have to take the band off again and put an open leg band on the bird later, when it is grown.

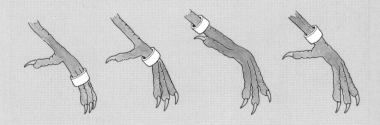

6|*Pull the band over the front toes and the longer back toe, then push it higher, over the shorter back toe.*

Understanding Parakeets

If you want to be able to interpret and understand your parakeets' habits, characteristics, and behavior and motor patterns (see How-To, page 62), it helps to become familiar with their typical behavior in the wild. The following material deals primarily with the life of the Australian parakeet species in their natural habitat, because these are the species that have been observed most closely.

Youth

The length of time young birds stay with their parents varies with the parakeet species. In species that brood several times a year—such as budgerigars, cockatiels, and eastern rosellas—the independent young birds wander away with other birds of their age as soon as the parents begin to brood again. In flocks, they practice and perfect their innate abilities, explore their environment, and accumulate experience in dealing with others of their kind. After only a few months, they reach sexual maturity themselves and begin to mate.

In parakeet species that breed only once a year—such as the regent parakeet, superb parakeet, and princess parakeet—the young birds stay longer with their parents. Often they become sexually mature only in their second or third year.

Pair Formation

What often proves to be difficult for captive parakeets just happens naturally in the wild. In the flocks of young birds, many young males and females meet one another. They go hunting for food together; they rest in a flock in bushes and trees during the hot midday hours; and at night they sleep in close proximity. If a male feels attracted to a female, he approaches cautiously and sits as close as possible to his intended. If she tolerates his presence, he soon tries to make contact by cautiously tapping her on the shoulder with his beak. If he is not rejected, the two soon form a pair.

Pair Bonding

Once two birds have decided to pair, they deal with each other very cautiously at first. The male demonstrates his size and strength in efforts to impress the female and tries to feed her or groom her head feathers.

The female goes along hesitantly until being part of a twosome feels comfortable and natural to her. Vocalizations also are part of the bonding process. What to the human ear sounds like gentle chirping or quiet chatting, the parakeet perceives as the highly differentiated expression of its partner's sentiments, which it usually endorses. These compatible moods result in the frequent unison in which the two partners stretch, wash, yawn, take wing, or draw back from the flock.

Pair bonding varies in intensity among the various parakeet species. Although budgerigars are "married for life," the Asiatic psittaculid parakeets remain paired only for the length of a brooding period.

Bright red and deep blue are the dominant colors of the Pennant's parakeet.

Brooding Periods

In Australia there are parakeet species that have fixed brooding periods each year, and others whose nesting depends on favorable growing seasons. The pairs of parakeets with fixed periods for brooding usually separate from their flock and breed in spring or early summer—this corresponds to the climate in central Europe in midsummer. At this time there are enough half-ripened seeds available; they are important in the development of the young.

Parakeets that live in dry, hot central Australia have no set brooding

57

times, because in this part of the country there are no fixed rainy seasons in the year. If rain falls, the birds start brooding at once, because they can use the plants that will appear to feed their young. If the vegetation remains satisfactory, the first brood is followed by a second, sometimes even a third. These parakeets brood in colonies, and at times there are two or three brooding hollows in a single tree. The pairs provide a stimulus for each other by their preparations for brooding and courtship; this puts the females more quickly in a mood to brood.

Brooding Preliminaries

The preparations for brooding always begin with the search for a suitable nesting site, which varies in appearance depending on the parakeet species. Most parakeet species prefer hollows in trees for brooding. Many parakeets seek out tree hollows high

above the ground, while other species brood right above ground level. Some like to nest in tree hollows almost 10 feet (3 m) deep, and others are happy with scantily roofed substitutes. Many parakeets are contented with a nest hollow in a tree trunk that is lying on the ground; others brood in the abandoned nests of owls or starlings. The golden-shouldered parakeet, for example, broods exclusively in the nests of a certain species of termite.

Usually it is the male who hunts out a nest hollow and shows it to the female. The female slips inside and tests the proposition. If the site passes inspection, the female gets to work in the hollow, if necessary using her bill to enlarge the nest cavity, entry hole, and inside area. The wood waste produced in this way is used as nesting material. Only the scarlet-chested parakeet pads its hollow with leaves, which it transports by sticking them into its rump feathers.

Courtship and Mating

Among all parakeets, courtship begins with the feeding of the female (see Feeding of Mate, page 63) and the male's efforts to impress her. Drawing himself up to his full height, he often struts around the female or back and forth in front of her. While so doing, many males raise their wings and spread their tail or move it from side to side. Usually this is accompanied by a narrowing of the pupils, with the iris becoming clearly visible. If the female is being fed, she bows before the male, her wings trembling slightly, in the begging posture of young birds. If she is ready to mate, she lifts her tail, lays her head far back, and thus entices the male to come closer. During copulation (see drawing, page 51), the male mounts the female's back and holds firmly to her feathers with his bill.

A parakeet brings one foot under a wing and lifts the foot to scratch its tiny head. (Drawing: Eastern rosella)

Depending on the species, courtship also includes special demonstration flights by the male, stimulating vocalizations, vigorous nods of the head, and—always—the display of striking color markings.

Brooding

Sitting on the eggs is the female's job. As a rule, she starts brooding after she has laid the second egg. During this period, she is fed by the male. In many species, the male feeds the female at the nest's entry hole, transferring the food from his crop; in others, the male entices the female from the nest hollow and feeds her outside on a branch. Occasionally both birds fly a short way together before the female returns to her clutch. Many males keep watch near the nest when they are not foraging for food; others fly around with their fellows and come to the nest only once an hour for feeding.

Once the young have hatched, they are fed by the female for the first few days, then the male shares in the task. From then on, both parents at times go out to search for food. If they return to the nest together, the male feeds the young birds first, then the female takes over.

Nest Hygiene

Parakeets, like all other parrots, do not keep their nest clean. We know that among many songbirds, the parents eat the droppings of their young or carry them out of the nest. Some parakeets have been shown to live in an advantageous symbiosis (See Glossary) with small butterflies. The caterpillars of these butterflies hatch from their eggs in the nest hollow of the parakeets and subsist on the nestlings' excrement. This astonishing symbiotic relationship was observed in detail in the golden-shouldered parakeet. In its nesting chamber, inside a

Parakeets love having their mate scratch their head. This not only promotes good hygiene, but also strengthens pair bonding. (Drawing: Canary-winged parakeet)

termite mound, were found caterpillars that not only kept the nest free of excrement, but even cleaned the feet and feathers of the young birds. It remains unclear how the butterflies determine the right moment for laying their eggs. If the caterpillars hatch before the birds, they die of starvation. If they hatch after the birds, they also starve, because the young birds will leave the nest while the caterpillars still need the bird droppings for food.

The Nestling Period

In many parakeet species, the independent young stay with their parents until the next brooding period. Usually this family unit lives by itself, but at times it bands together with another (for example, the Bourke's parakeet, Pennant's parakeet, and eastern ro-

Among Derbyan parakeets (Psittacula alexandri fasciata) feeding a mate is part of the brooding phase.

sella). The red-rumped parakeet, elegant parakeet, and blue-winged parakeet, live in swarms of several hundred birds. Among red-rumped parakeets there even exists a regular pecking order, which presupposes that the birds in the swarm know each other precisely. The subordinate parakeet has to give way to the one with higher standing in the hierarchy. The females acquire the rank of their partner. The central Australian species travel together in swarms only when food and water are scarce, in order to search for better living conditions; otherwise, they live together in smaller groups.

Bathing and Drinking

Many parakeets come to their watering place in the morning and evening, often even after dark; others come several times a day or even hourly. In addition to natural bodies of water, livestock ponds in pastures often serve as sources of drinking water. In areas where water is scarce, parakeets drink and bathe in the dew that forms in the grass after cold nights. If rain falls, many enjoy letting the rain wash them. An exception is the Bourke's parakeet, which almost never bathes.

Watch parakeets while they drink, and you will see that almost all of them give the impression of being slightly nervous. Many stand submerged up to their abdomen when they drink, while others take a few hasty swallows and fly off again. The golden-shouldered parakeet is particularly timid. It lands high up in a tree overlooking a watering place and descends slowly, branch by branch. Often an entire hour passes before it dares to drink a few drops swiftly, only to fly away again at once.

Sedentary Bird, Visitant, or Migrant?

The parakeet species that live in areas near the coast with lush vegetation are sedentary, or nonmigratory, birds; that is, they live permanently in an area and move only a few miles. In dry regions such as those of central Australia, parakeets travel around in swarms, looking for food and water. They are visitants, and they lead a predominantly nomadic life. The Australian blue-winged parakeet, golden-bellied parakeet, and swift parakeet are migratory birds; they spend the breeding season in summer on the island of Tasmania and return across Bass Strait to the mainland for the winter.

Enemies and Dangers

Originally, parakeets were endangered primarily by birds of prey. Their way of life has adapted itself to this threat. Many live in tall trees with a broad view of the surroundings, so that they can quickly warn each other and take flight. In the leaves of trees and on the ground, parakeets are well concealed by the colors of their feathers. They rely on this camouflage too often, however, and go in search of food without particular caution. Because they have developed no natural warning mechanisms to protect them from the cats, foxes, and other small imported predators, they frequently are easy prey for these animals. A particular threat is the starling, a bird also imported and now common in Australia. It confiscates nest hollows for its own use, and these nests often are in short supply anyway, owing to the dwindling numbers of trees.

There is an additional danger for parakeet species that are described as synanthropic—that is, they survive in areas cultivated by man. Often these birds alight in huge flocks on agricultural acreage, and the methods used to control them are usually ruthless. In addition, the parakeet population is endangered by long-lasting periods of drought, brushfires, and—above all—the progressive destruction of the natural countryside, for example, the clearing of wooded areas.

Many parakeets are threatened with extinction because of the progressive destruction of the natural landscape in their native countries. Concerted efforts to breed endangered species can contribute to their preservation. Some extremely threatened species soon may exist only as captive-bred birds.

HOW-TO
The Language of Parakeets

On these pages, typical behavioral and motor patterns, all of which you can observe repeatedly in your parakeets, are illustrated and described. If you know what they mean, you will understand your birds better and be able to read the state of their health.

1|Parakeets like to stretch thoroughly after they rest.

Stretching
Drawing 1
A parakeet almost always will stretch thoroughly after it has paused for rest. The stretching motions probably are intended to overcome fatigue. First the parakeet slightly spreads its wings above its back, then it stretches itself by extending one leg and the wing on the same side toward the back. As the leg is drawn back into place, the foot usually curls up like a fist.

Feather Grooming
Drawing 2
Parakeets devote themselves to grooming their plumage several times a day. With the exception of the head area, they can reach all parts of their body with their bill. They draw all the feathers through the bill to smoothe them, even the long tail feathers. Using the bill, they take a secretion from the preen gland, or uropygial gland—an organ in the shape of a ringlike crease, located under the plumage on the lower back, slightly above the tail feathers—and spread it on their plumage. This oily coating keeps the feathers from becoming completely soaked when it rains or when the bird bathes. In the same way, the oil protects the feathers from being dried out by wind and heat. The birds turn their head 180° and rub it on the preen gland, because they cannot, of course, reach their head with their bill. To preen the head feathers, many parakeets also bring one foot up underneath the wing to reach the head.

Social grooming is limited in many parakeet species—rosellas in particular—to the head area. Other species, however, groom each other's entire plumage. Social grooming not only keeps the birds clean, but is also an essential element of pair bonding.

Yawning
Drawing 3
We humans are not the only animals that yawn; parakeets yawn too, their beaks gaping wide. Yawning is not a sign of exhaustion, however, but of oxygen deficiency. If your parakeets live indoors, make sure that enough fresh air can circulate (see page 16), without causing a draft. Parakeets have a more sensitive reaction to stale air than humans do.

Mate Feeding
Drawing 4
Among most parakeet species, the feeding of a mate is an essential part of pair formation. During courtship, this behavior should be viewed as a prelude to copulation. The female, often bent over in a begging attitude, approaches the male and allows him to feed her. Only if she is satisfactorily fed—even though feeding may be only suggested by billing—will she be willing to mate. Later, during the brooding period and the raising of her young, the female will spend the bulk of her time in the nest hollow, dependent on the male to bring food for her and the nestlings. The male forages for food near the nest hollow and transfers it from his crop to the female at the nest's

2|Parakeets preen themselves extensively every day.

3│*When yawning, parakeets open their beak wide.*

entry hole. Many males also entice their mate to come out onto a nearby branch and feed her there.

In many parakeet species with especially close pair bonding, the feeding of a mate also can be observed outside the breeding period, throughout the entire year. Cockatiels are an exception. Because both partners take turns sitting on the eggs and feeding the young, these birds do not feed their mates.

Billing
Drawing 5
Billing is also a type of feeding behavior, without any actual transfer of food. During courtship, it serves to strengthen the bonding of a pair and to prepare for brooding. Billing is a bird's ritualized way of suggesting the act of feeding its mate. In some parakeet species, it also is used to pacify a mate.

Sleeping and Resting
When parakeets sleep, they sit quietly on one leg with their eyes closed and their feathers slightly ruffled. The other leg is bent and drawn up into the feathers on the abdomen. Quite often the birds also turn their heads to the back and stick their beaks into the back feathers (see drawing, page 26). During periods of rest, the birds of a swarm maintain a certain distance from each other when sitting on branches or perches. This space is called the individual distance. If the space is too small, either an assault results or the animal departs, its fellow

having moved too close for comfort. Individual distance is suspended, however, in cold weather. Then the birds sit

5│*Billing is a way of strengthening the bond between a pair.*

close together, their feathers ruffled up, to prevent heat loss. The ruffled feathers retain air, which acts as an insulating layer between the body and the outside air.

During the brooding and nestling periods the male parakeet feeds the female— often at the nest's entry hole.

4│*Feeding a mate: The male regurgitates food for the female from his crop.*

63

Parakeet Species

In this chapter, you will find important pointers on the appearance and care of some popular parakeet species. The majority of the chosen species are listed in Appendix II of CITES. This means that these species may be bought or sold, provided all legal regulations are observed.

Species Conservation Through Breeding?

Many parakeet species are threatened with extinction in their homeland by the destruction of their natural habitats. The indiscriminate clearing of wooded areas results in the destruction of trees used for nesting, trees whose numbers are dwindling in any case. Despite the Washington Convention on Species Conservation (see page 24), poachers throughout the world are continuing to capture protected parakeets. The power of government authorities rarely extends to the remote regions where the birds live.

Conscientious bird fanciers, therefore, firmly refuse to keep parakeets that were captured and removed from their natural habitat or whose origin is not absolutely clear. You should buy only captive-bred parakeets! Perhaps in a few years the entire market for parakeets can be supplied by bird breeders.

My tip: If you want to breed birds successfully, provide optimum living conditions. This is the only way to ensure that the offspring are healthy. If you are not interested in bird breeding, perhaps because you have only a single bird, then lend your parakeet to a breeder who needs a suitable sex partner for a parakeet.

About the Profiles

In the preceding chapters, you were presented with general information about the nature, housing, care, proper feeding, and breeding of parakeets. On the following pages, you will find photos and descriptions of popular parakeets, accompanied by the following information:

Distinguishing features: The most prominent characteristics of the plumage of the particular parakeet species are given. If the species has subspecies, the features cited refer to the nominate form (see Glossary). As a rule, the subspecies are cared for in the same way as the species.

Habitat: These are the regions where the bird prefers to live.

Behavior: Typical patterns of behavior in the wild that provide care pointers.

Keeping: Special tips on keeping and breeding.

Pointer: Other important data on breeding the particular species—such as the requisite size of the nest box, sexual maturity, incubation time, and the size of the leg band required by law—are found in the table on page 88.

The parakeets chosen for inclusion are primarily species listed in Appendix II of CITES (see page 24) and thus available in pet stores or from breeders.

Almost all parakeet species nest in hollows or cavities. The appearance of these nesting sites varies considerably, however. They may be hollows in trees, cracks in rocks, decayed branches, loam walls, or even termites' nests.

An eastern rosella that lives in the wild, shown here entering a nest hollow.

Rosellas

1|Stanley parakeet   2|Pale-headed rosella

Australia

Australia is the land of parrots and parakeets. Over 30 different species of parakeets live there. On the following pages, we present to you the best-loved and most frequently kept Australian parakeets.

1 Stanley Parakeet
Western rosella
Platycercus icterotis
Subspecies: Western Stanley parakeet (*P. i. icterotis*), eastern Stanley parakeet (*P. i. xanthogenys*). Same care.
Distinguishing features: Male: Yellow cheek patch; head, breast, and abdomen red; back and wings black, edged in green; terminal segments of pinions blue. Female: Paler cheek patch; breast and head green and red; frontal band red. Young: Predominantly green; no cheek patch.
Habitat: Coastal regions, pastures, arable land.

Behavior: Trusting, peaceable; close pair bonding; very lively; much climbing; no gnawing; pleasant voice.
Keeping: Needs bathing facilities constantly available. Isolate brooding pairs, which are aggressive; usually only one brood per year.

2 Pale-headed Rosella
Platycercus adscitus
Subspecies: Blue-cheeked rosella (*P. a. adscitus*), pale-headed or mealy rosella (*P. a. palliceps*). Same care.
Distinguishing features: Male and female alike. Cheek patch white; upper part of head almost white; throat, bend of wing, and abdomen blue; breast yellowish blue; back black, edged in yellow. Young: Paler; wavy marking on head.
Habitat: Subtropical and tropical lowland regions with trees.
Behavior: Forages for food pri-

marily in trees; grips food with the foot; loves to bathe.
Keeping: Isolate brooding pairs, which are aggressive; keep no other *Platycercus* species in the next enclosure.

3 Eastern Rosella
Golden-mantled rosella
Platycercus eximius
Subspecies: Red rosella (*P. e. eximius*), *P. e. diemenensis*, Cecilia's or golden-mantled rosella (*P. e. ceciliae*). Same care.
Distinguishing features: Male and female alike. Cheek patch white; head and breast red; abdomen greenish yellow; rump green; back and wings black, edged with yellow. Young: Nape of the neck and crown green.
Habitat: Originally, open savannas; today, cultivated areas.
Behavior: Unless nesting, lives in small groups; in large flock in

Rosellas

3 | *Eastern rosella*

4 | *Pennant's parakeet*

winter; quarrels common among males.
Keeping: Preferably, keep one pair alone in the enclosure; loud voice; breeds easily, usually twice a year.

4 Pennant's Parakeet
Crimson rosella
Platycercus elegans
Subspecies: Southern Pennant's parakeet (*P. e. elegans*), northern Pennant's parakeet (*P. e. nigres-cens*), *P. e. fleurieuensis*, Adelaide rosella (*P. e. adelaidae*), *P. e. sub-adelaidae*, yellow rosella (*P. e. flaveolus*). Plumage colors vary; same care.
Distinguishing features: Male and female alike. Crimson; cheek patch blue-violet; terminal segments of pinions blue; back and wings black, edged in red. Young: Green; crown red.

Habitat: Prefers dense forests.
Behavior: Hardly shy of humans; much scratching in the ground; likes gnawing; uses foot to bring food to beak; hardy. Forms family units after brooding. Pleasant voice.
Keeping: Isolate brooding pairs, which are aggressive; usually only one brood per year.

Red-backed Parakeets

1 Red-rumped Parakeet

Red-backed parakeet
Psephotus haematonotus
Distinguishing features: Male: Rump bright red; cheeks and back bluish green; upper head and nape grass-green; outer vanes of primaries pale blue; abdomen and median coverts yellow. Female: Gray-green plumage; rump green; abdomen and undertail coverts white; underside yellowish. Young: Colors more subdued; rump of young males slightly red.
Habitat: Open eucalyptus savannas; gardens and fields.
Behavior: Strong pair bonding; gregarious; hierarchy and pecking order exist in flocks.
Keeping: Pleasant voice. Isolate brooding pairs, which are aggressive. Likes to spend time on the ground; cover aviary floor with soil and grass. Sensitive to cold; room temperature at least 59°F (15°C) during brooding. Prefers natural tree trunk as brooding site (8 inches [20 cm] in diameter, 24 inches [60 cm] high).

2 Mulga Parakeet

Psephotus varius
Distinguishing features: Plumage colors vary, depending on geographic range; shades of red predominate. Male: Breast and head bluish green; crown patch red; frontal band yellow; shoulders, abdomen, undertail coverts, and thighs yellow, with orange marking. Female: Frontal band orange; crown patch light red; head, breast, and upper back greenish to light brown; abdomen lime-green. Young: Colors more subdued; some red on young males' abdomens.

1 | Pair of red-rumped parakeets

Red-backed Parakeets

2 *Mulga parakeet*

3 *Psephotus haematogaster*

Habitat: Dry bush, grassland with few trees.

Behavior: Lives in pairs or small groups; forms family units after brooding; strong pair bonding.

Keeping: Soft voice; cover aviary floor with soil and grass because this bird spends much time scraping on the ground; sensitive to cold; room temperature at least 59°F (15°C) during brooding period. Prefers natural tree trunk as brooding site (8 inches [20 cm] in diameter, 24 inches [60 cm] high).

3 *Psephotus haematogaster*

Subspecies: *P. h. haematogaster*, *P. h. haematorrhous*, *P. h. pallescens*, *P. h. narethae*. Plumage colors vary in intensity; same care.

Distinguishing features: Male: Pale gray to brown plumage; breast has yellow markings; crown, lore, and terminal segments of pinions blue; abdomen yellow with conspicuous red patch. Female: Bill smaller; red patch on abdomen is paler. Females and young birds have a white stripe on the underwing.

Habitat: Dry savannas and grassland thinly covered with trees.

Behavior: Extremely playful: They roll on the floor with their mate like cats at play; they enjoy playing with rocks and branches; frequent mutual grooming of feathers; if agitated, they nod their beak vehemently, with their forehead feathers standing on end.

Keeping: Very quarrelsome; keep only one pair, alone; prefers natural tree trunk as nesting site (8 inches [20 cm] in diameter, 24 inches [60 cm] high); room temperature at least 59°F (15°C) during brooding.

Grass Parakeets

1 Scarlet-chested parakeet

2 Elegant parakeets

1 Scarlet-chested Parakeet
Splendid grass parakeet
Neophema splendida
Distinguishing features: Male: Head blue; throat dark blue; primaries light blue; upper side and tail green; abdomen and underside of tail yellow. Female: Breast yellowish green; head grayish brown; forehead, cheeks, lore blue. Young: Colors more subdued than those of female; young males have more blue and isolated red breast feathers.
Habitat: Dry regions with eucalyptus bushes and spinifex grass.
Behavior: Peaceful, sheltered way of life; drinks little; female lines nest with leaves.

Keeping: Develops trust gradually; melodious voice; aviary floor should be covered with a layer of soil and planted with grass and small shrubs; highly sensitive to cold and damp.

2 Elegant Parakeet
Neophema elegans
Distinguishing features: Male: Upper side gold to olive green; underside yellowish with orange patch on abdomen; blue frontal band, above which a thin light-blue stripe extends as far as the eyes; secondaries blue; primaries dark violet. Female: Stump olive green; no stripe above the frontal band and no patch on abdomen. Young: Resemble female; no frontal band.

Habitat: Open countryside, grassland with bushes.
Behavior: Lives in flock; spends much time on the ground and in dense scrub undergrowth.
Keeping: As for scarlet-chested parakeet.

70

Grass Parakeets

3 | Turquoise parakeet

4 | Blue-winged parakeet

3 Turquoise Parakeet

Turquoisine parakeet
Neophema pulchella
Distinguishing features: Male: Face and upper wing coverts blue; forehead dark blue; lower wing coverts and outer edge of pinions dark blue; wing band red; upper side green; underside yellow. Female: Colors more subdued; less blue on face; no wing band. Young: Resemble female; young males have somewhat more blue on face; wing band is discernible.
Habitat: Hilly, densely wooded regions, steep rocky valleys.
Behavior: Trusting; lives in flocks; extremely timid near water; female often carries strips of leaves into nest.

Keeping: As for scarlet-chested parakeet.

4 Blue-winged Parakeet

Neophema chrysostoma
Distinguishing features: Male: Upper side olive green; blue frontal band with light border; lore yellow; breast green; abdomen orange, mostly during brooding, then lighter; secondaries brilliant deep blue; primaries black with narrow white edges. Female: Colors more subdued; secondaries dark brown. Young: Colors more subdued; no frontal band.
Habitat: Heath, open pastures, cultivated land, coastal regions.
Behavior: Very gregarious;

peaceable nature; spends much time on the ground; broods in groups of up to ten pairs.
Keeping: As for turquoise parakeet.

Budgerigar

1 | Budgerigars with plumage coloring in the wild

blue. Female: Cere beige to brownish. Young: Colors paler; wavy marking on head extends to cere.

Habitat: Semidesert regions with some grass; along river courses where eucalyptus trees grow.

Behavior: Pairs bond closely; they feed their mates even when not brooding; they live in pairs in a group or, during migration, in large flocks; the female is dominant and males are reluctant to attack a female; they breed after periods of rainfall.

Keeping: Exceedingly sociable; a bird kept singly becomes closely attached to a human and even learns to mimic words or short sentences; preferably, however, keep a pair. In large community aviaries they can brood together.

Caution: Keep loners out of a brooding aviary, because they often cause trouble. Allow only two broods per year.

2 Cockatiel
Nymphicus hollandicus
Distinguishing features: Male: Delicate gray plumage, sometimes also grayish blue or brownish gray; upper tail coverts silvery gray; conspicuous white feathers on outer wing coverts; throat, cheeks, and forehead bright lemon yellow; cheek patch reddish orange; the crest feathers rise from the yellow forehead plumage, the front feathers shorter and yellow and the back ones longer and gray; cere gray-brown. Female: Yellow mask and cheek patch more subdued in color and overlaid with gray; underside of tail feathers horizontally striped. Young: Like the female; the tail is shorter.

1 Budgerigar
Shell parakeet, budgie, parakeet
Melopsittacus undulatus
Distinguishing features: Budgerigars have been bred in many color varieties; the wild form is light green. Male: Forehead and face yellow; six black dots on the throat near the breast; cheeks have some small bluish violet feathers; wavy or shell-like marking on back of head, back, and wing coverts, created by black feathers edged in yellow; cere

Cockatiel

Bourke's Parakeet

2│Cockatiel

3│Bourke's parakeet

Habitat: Arid regions, semideserts, and bushy steppes, in particular along river courses where eucalyptus trees grow.

Behavior: Lives in pairs in a group; close pair bonding but no feeding of mate, because both parents take turns sitting; male "sings" during courtship.

Keeping: Pleasant pet, peaceable and sweet-tempered; can be tamed and often will learn to whistle; keeping pairs is advisable because single birds often scream loudly; breeds readily in large community aviaries; allow birds to brood only twice a year.

3 Bourke's Parakeet
Neopsephotus bourkii
Distinguishing features: Male: Head and breast brownish pink, changing to old rose toward the abdomen; blue frontal band; undertail coverts light blue; tail and pinions blue; back feathers brown-black, edged with light brown to beige. Female: Frontal band only intimated; pink shades are more subdued. Young: Like female; in some males the blue frontal band is sketchy.
Habitat: Open bushy steppes, regions with mulga acacias.
Behavior: Usually lives in pairs in groups or, during migration, in flocks; usually flies just above ground level; spends much time on the ground; active chiefly in the early morning, before sunset, and on bright moonlit nights; bathes rarely; breeds after periods of rainfall.
Keeping: Pleasant pet; does not gnaw or scream; chirping has a charming sound; trusting; agreeable; when not brooding can be kept with members of its own species and some finches (Australian grass finches, Gouldians, zebra finches, etc.); isolate pairs during brooding; allow to brood only twice a year.

Polytelis Parakeets

2 | Regent parakeet

1 | Pair of superb parakeets

1 Superb Parakeet
Polytelis swainsonii
Distinguishing features: Male: Green plumage, with underside darker than upper side; crown, forehead, cheeks, and throat sunny yellow; bill and a crescent-shaped badge around the throat red; outer primaries blue. Female: Colors paler; no yellow in the head area and no red badge; only the outer tail feathers are red. Young: Resemble female; young males are somewhat deeper green.
Habitat: Narrow wooded strips along river courses with tall eucalyptus trees, damp steppes.

Behavior: Small groups of about ten birds live together even when brooding; males form small troops that they leave repeatedly to get food for their mates; they imitate other birds' voices.
Keeping: Loud piercing voice. Otherwise, as for regent parakeet.

2 Regent Parakeet
Polytelis anthopeplus
Distinguishing features: Male: Predominantly yellow; back olive green; large wing coverts black; median wing coverts and bill red. Female: Colors more subdued; predominantly olive green. Young: Like female; males more yellow than olive green.
Habitat: In eastern Australia, regent parakeets live concealed in bushy steppes with dense vegetation and eucalyptus trees. In western Australia they live chiefly in wheat-growing regions.
Behavior: Quite peaceable; lives in groups of up to 20 birds; the best flier among the Australian parakeets.
Keeping: Desirable aviary birds, because they are trusting and agreeable; pleasant voices; take only spray baths; two to three pairs can also live and brood in a large community aviary; one brood per year.

74

Red-capped Parakeets

3 Princess parakeet

4 Red-capped parakeets

3 Princess of Wales Parakeet
Alexandra's parakeet
Polytelis alexandrae
Distinguishing features: Male: Crown and forehead light blue; throat and front of neck pink; underside light gray; upper side olive green; wing coverts greenish yellow; rump bluish violet; thighs and lower flanks pink; pinions light blue; outer tail feathers bluish gray, edged with pink. Female: Colors more subdued; tail shorter; somewhat more slender. Young: Resemble female.
Habitat: As nomads, they always live near watering sites and trees where they can nest; predominantly desertlike regions.
Behavior: Spends much time on the ground; leads a reclusive life and steers clear of humans; broods after periods of rainfall.
Keeping: Popular aviary bird because of its gentle, fearless nature; agreeable and trusting; its cries, however, frequently are loud. Otherwise, as for regent parakeet.

4 Red-capped Parakeet
Pileated parakeet
Purpureicephalus spurius
Distinguishing features: Male: Elongated, only slightly hooked upper bill; forehead, crown, thighs, and undertail coverts red; cheeks and throat yellow; breast and abdomen bright bluish violet; upper side yellowish green to dark green. Female: Colors more subdued; head reddish green or green; breast and abdomen grayish blue-violet. Young: Colors more subdued than in female; isolated red forehead feathers.
Habitat: Dense eucalyptus forests or regions where eucalyptus is plentiful.
Behavior: Lives in pairs or in small groups; uses its long bill to extract pollen and nectar from flowers and seeds from eucalyptus pods.
Keeping: Quite lively and curious, but timid; metallic rattling voice; strong urge to gnaw, so provide plenty of branches; bathes frequently and with great enthusiasm; needs abundant opportunity to fly.

Ringneck Parakeets

1 Mallee ringneck

2 Bauer's rosella

1 Mallee Ringneck
Barnardius barnardi
Subspecies: Barnard's ringneck
(*B. b. barnardi*), Cloncurry ringneck
(*B. b. macgillivrayi*), Lake Eyre Barnard's ringneck (*B. b. whitei*). Same
care.
Distinguishing features: Male:
Dark green with red frontal band
and light blue accents on cheeks,
shoulders, and wing coverts; yellow
collar on nape. Female: Colors
somewhat more subdued. Young:
Reddish orange frontal band.
Habitat: Eucalyptus scrub, open
forest.
Behavior: Lives in seclusion in
the shade of deciduous trees; uses
foot to bring food to bill.

Keeping: Quiet aviary bird; pair
formation creates problems at
times; quickly separate any pairs
that are not getting along; prefers
natural tree trunk as brooding hollow (14 inches [35 cm] in diameter,
39 inches [100 cm] high); can breed
twice a year.

2 Port Lincoln Ringneck
Barnardius zonarius
Subspecies: Bauer's ringneck
(*B. z. zonarius*), collared or "twenty-
eight" parakeet (*B. z. semitorqua-
tus*), *B. z. dundasi*, *B. z. occiden-
talis*, and *B. z. myrtae*. Same care.
Distinguishing features: Male:
Blackish brown head with bluish violet cheeks; bill light horn color; collar light yellow; wing coverts and
breast green; abdomen dark yellow.
Female: Colors more subdued.

Young: Colors even more subdued
Habitat: Regions where eucalyptus grows, parks, and coastal forests.
Behavior: Usually found only in
pairs, never in swarms; lives near
wheat-growing regions; in inland regions has no fixed brooding periods.
Keeping: Needs a great deal of
opportunity to gnaw and to fly. Aggressive toward *Platycercus* and
other *Barnardius* species.

New Zealand Parakeets or Kakarikis

New Zealand

New Zealand is the home of two parakeet species that now are common worldwide and quite popular as aviary birds: *Cyanoramphus novaezelandiae* and *Cyanoramphus auriceps*. It seems incredible that both birds have been commercially available only since the 1970s.

3 Yellow-fronted Parakeet
Cyanoramphus auriceps
Distinguishing features: Male: Plumage dark green, lighter toward the head; bill blue; frontal band red; forehead yellow; red patch on each side of the rump; primaries and secondaries blue. Female: Frontal band narrower; less yellow on the forehead. Young: Colors more subdued; short tail.
Habitat: Regions where trees grow, open forests.
Behavior: Cheerful; great need for exercise; lives in small groups; avoids open countryside; cries like those of red-fronted parakeet, but pleasantly low; frequently appears along with red-fronted parakeet.
Keeping: Popular because of its lively activity; close pair bonding; pairs defend each other and scream incessantly if they are separated; needs soil on the aviary floor, if possible planted with grass and small shrubs; bathing facilities should be available at all times; protection from sun necessary on hot days; room temperature about 64°F (18°C) during brooding period. These birds prefer a natural tree trunk as a brooding hollow (10 inches [25 cm] in diameter, 24 inches [60 cm] high). New nest box required for second brood in a year.

3 | Pair of yellow-fronted New Zealand parakeets

Similar species: Red-fronted parakeet (*Cyanoramphus novaezelandiae*).

Males and females have deep-green plumage. The crown, forehead, and a small patch behind each eye and on each side of the rump are bright red; the primaries are blue-violet. The female has a smaller head, and the bill and patch behind each eye are slightly smaller. In young birds, the red coloring is less brilliant.

Red-fronted parakeets inhabit primarily well-wooded regions, but they also have adapted to life on the ground. They are extremely agile fliers; their cries are reminiscent of goats' constant bleating.

77

Quaker Parakeet

1|Quaker parakeet

Narrow-billed Parakeet

2|Canary-winged parakeets

South America

The South American parakeets are not quite as popular as the Australian species, because the color of their plumage generally is less eye-catching. Many of them, however, have an extremely lovable nature. They are lively and curious, and in captivity they often become tame and trusting.

1 Quaker Parakeet
Monk parakeet
Myiopsitta monachus
Distinguishing features: Male and female alike. Cheeks and neck light gray; breast edged with white; crown and forehead light gray with slight tinge of green; upper side grass-green; abdomen greenish yellow; primaries black and blue; elongated bill horn-colored.
Young: Forehead and crown deeper green.
Habitat: Regions with bushes and tall brooding trees.
Behavior: The only parrot species that builds a nest in tall trees; these birds, which brood in colonies, make

their nests side by side; each nest consists of a brooding room and an antechamber.
Keeping: They can be kept in pairs in community aviaries, but no unpaired parakeets should be in the aviary; loud voices. Good breeders if a sturdy wire mesh foundation is provided, on which they can fix the twigs for building their nests; they seldom accept nest boxes.

2 Canary-winged Parakeet
Brotogeris versicolorus chiriri
A subspecies of the white-winged parakeet (*Brotogeris versicolorus*).
Distinguishing features: Male and female alike. Green plumage, green secondary coverts; thin bluish white eye ring; light beige beak. Young quickly acquire these features.
Habitat: Primarily the outskirts of forests and riverbanks where trees grow.
Behavior: Lives in a swarm; breeds in tree hollows or in termite nests in trees; pairs occasionally screech in alternation; during brooding both partners sleep in the nest box.

edge-tailed Parakeet

Nanday Parakeet

3|*Mitred conure*

4|*Nanday parakeet, or black-headed conure*

Keeping: Trusting; do not house brooding pairs in an enclosure next to *Aratinga* species, because they do not get along.

3 Mitred Conure
Aratinga mitrata
Distinguishing features: Male and female alike. Moss-green; breast and abdomen lighter; forehead, crown, cheeks, and lore red; individual red feathers distributed over entire body with the exception of the wings; white eye ring; light horn-colored beak. Young: Green with narrow frontal band.
Habitat: Dry forests, semiopen terrain, arable land.
Behavior: Frequently leads nomadic life; lives in pairs or in small groups; good flier, able to cover long distances at high altitude, emitting loud cries; curious and quite lively.
Keeping: Trusting; playful; mimics noises; loud voice; likes to gnaw and bathe; double wire mesh essential between the compartments,

because these birds quarrel with their neighbors.

4 Nanday Parakeet
Black-headed conure
Nandayus nenday
Distinguishing features: Male and female alike. Upper part of head, face, chin, cheeks, and bill black; eye ring white; throat and breast pale blue; thighs red; remaining plumage green; underside yellowish green. Young quickly come to resemble parents.
Habitat: Not tied to specific types of landscapes.

Behavior: Broods in colonies; males often do guard duty next to the nest, screeching all the while; after breeding, lives in swarms, often along with Quaker parakeets; lives near wheat-growing regions.
Keeping: Four to five pairs can be kept and allowed to brood in a large common aviary; likes to gnaw, climb, and bathe; loud voice; separate the aviary compartments with double wire mesh, because they quarrel with neighboring birds; hand-raised Nanday parakeets are highly suitable for keeping in a pair as pets.

79

Ringneck Parakeets (*Psittacula*)

1 | *Plumhead parakeet*

2 | *Mustached parakeet*

Asia

The ringneck parakeets (*Psittacula*) living in Asia are noteworthy for their strikingly marked plumage. They have a colored neck ring or a pronounced stripe running through the chin region. In many, the head is brilliantly colored. Psittaculid parakeets are exceptions in that they do not form lasting bonds with a mate. After brooding, the pairs separate once more.

1 Plumhead Parakeet
Psittacula cyanocephala
Distinguishing features: Male: Head plum-colored; upper bill light orange; the black chin stripe merges into the narrow collar ring, beneath which the plumage is delicate turquoise; upper side green; underside yellowish green; reddish brown stripe on the lesser coverts. Female: Head light grayish violet; collar ring dull yellow; no wing stripe; upper beak light yellow. Young: Colors paler than in female.
Habitat: Woods near arable land—grainfields and fruit plantations, for example.
Behavior: Live in a swarm; search jointly for food; sleep in large trees and constantly make their presence known with great vocal effort; no lasting pair bonding.
Keeping: Offer them ample opportunities for climbing; loud voices; sensitive to freezing temperatures; breed readily, but not always successful in raising young; hand-raising is frequently necessary.

2 Mustached Parakeet
Psittacula alexandri fasciata
Distinguishing features: Male: Upper side olive green; head gray with tinge of blue; breast dark pink; wide black chin stripe; narrow black stripe joining the eyes; red upper bill. Female: Breast salmon pink; head and face light blue-green; black upper bill. Young: Green; suggestion of black chin and eye stripes; red bill, turning black after about five weeks and later—

80

Ringneck Parakeets (*Psittacula*)

3 | *Ringneck parakeet (pair)*

in mature males—becoming red again.

Habitat: Low plains and gentle slopes in mountainous areas.

Behavior: Lives in a swarm; no permanent pair bonding; during courtship, male and female sit side by side and trill, turning their heads constantly.

Keeping: Loud voice; otherwise, as for ringneck parakeet.

3 Ringneck Parakeet

Rose-ringed parakeet
Psittacula krameri

Subspecies: African ringneck parakeet (*P. k. krameri*), Indian ringneck parakeet (*P. k. manillensis*). Hard to tell apart; same care.

Distinguishing features: Male: Green plumage, which on the back of the head has a bluish tint; bill red; stripe on nape salmon red; neck ring black. Female: No neck ring and no stripe on nape. Young: Resemble female, but have a shorter tail.

Habitat: Originally forests, now, in addition, arable land, such as fields, plantations, and gardens.

Behavior: Lives in swarms; courtship behavior of males is distinctive; no lasting pair bonding.

Keeping: Highly gregarious, hence several pairs can be kept jointly in a large aviary; likes spray baths; sensitive to freezing temperatures.

Glossary

A

Aspergillosis
A fungal infection due to mold; has no known remedy. Life-threatening for parakeets. It is important to remove moldy food immediately!

B

Bergmann's Rule
According to this rule, the habitat determines the size of the birds within a species. For example, Pennant's parakeets that live in hot zones are smaller than those from temperate zones. The reason is that the larger Pennant's parakeets have a small body surface in relation to their body weight—body surface does not increase in proportion to weight. Consequently, the birds cannot give off much heat. On the other hand, small Pennant's parakeets have a large surface relative to their weight and can give off a great deal of heat. This explains why the smallest subspecies of the Pennant's parakeet lives in the hottest region of Australia.

Bill of the Parakeet
The upper bill of parakeets is connected to the skull bone by a movable joint. The lower bill can be shifted from side to side by means of a sliding joint. The great mobility of the bill results from this arrangement. If the bird is looked after appropriately, the horny substance (keratin) of the bill is continually being worn down. The bill appears to be scaling. This natural process is counterbalanced by the continued growth of the keratin in the bill. In almost all the species, filing ridges are located on the lower side of the tip of the upper bill. They afford the bill a better grip and simultaneously keep it sharp and smooth.

Brooding Temperature
For most parakeets, a temperature of 98.6°F (37°C) is ideal for brooding. Lower temperatures may delay the hatching of the young. It is sufficient if the room temperature for the birds is between 55° and 64°F (13°–18°C): Inside the nest box, the close contact with the female's body will provide the eggs with the required temperature of 98.6°F (37°C).

Building Permit
First, always determine whether a building permit is required for the construction of an outdoor aviary with a night shelter. This depends on the local building code.

C

Cere
The cere is located at the base of the beak and surrounds the nostrils, or nares. In many parakeet species, the cere is strikingly colored. In some species, the cere is also covered with fine feathers. It may also aid in sexing: Budgerigar males with the native coloring have a blue cere, while that of the females is brownish-beige.

Clutch
A nest of eggs or a brood of chicks.

Colony Brooders
These are parakeet species that brood in colonies in the wild. In captivity, however, they should be kept only in pairs, so that they have enough space and sufficient peace and quiet. Exceptions: Particularly peaceable parakeet species such as the budgerigar, gray-cheeked, or orange-flanked parakeet (*Brotogeris pyrrhopterus*), canary-winged parakeet, Quaker parakeet, and cockatiel. In sufficiently large aviaries or aviary compartments, any one of these species also can brood in groups.

Covert
A feather covering the bases of the quills of the wings and tail.

Crop
The pouched enlargement of the bird's gullet to soften and hold food.

D

Dimorphism
See Sexual Dimorphism.

Disturbance of the Peace
Many parakeet species (see profiles, pages 64 to 81) have particularly loud, shrill voices. If something should ever cause the birds to sound joint warning cries, your neighbors might experience considerable annoyance.

Down
Fine, soft feathers that cover the body of most newly hatched parakeets. In some species, the young are naked when hatched. The first down falls out after a few days and is replaced by new down feathers, which are denser and often different in color as well.

E

Egg Tooth
Calcareous thorn-shaped prominence on the upper bill of the young parakeet. Used in breaking its way out of the egg (see page 50). The egg tooth drops off five to seven days after the bird hatches.

Endoscopy
Surgical procedure to determine the sex of a parakeet. In my opinion, the birds should not be subjected to this operation. Experienced breeders can also tell the sex of their young birds by external features (see also, Sexing).

Ergot
In late summer or fall, the ergot fungus, a parasite that lives on wild grasses and grain, replaces the affected spikes or ears with ergot, a poisonous sclerotic body. Ergot may inadvertently be contained in any seed mix you buy. For this reason, spread the grains out, a portion at a time, and search through them to see whether ergot is present. It occurs predominantly in rye, occasionally also in wheat and oats. It is clearly larger than a seed of grain and is blackish in color. For humans, consumption of a small amount of ergot is not dangerous, but for small birds such as parakeets, a single ergot can be quite harmful.

F

Feet of the Parakeet
Parakeets have the parrots' typical climbing foot. The two toes in the middle point to the front, the two outer toes to the back. Just as the bill helps the feet during climbing, the feet also assist the beak during eating. Many parakeet species grip food firmly with one foot in order to get at it more easily with the beak. Anyone who keeps a budgerigar will have a chance to see the bird hold spray millet firmly in its foot and draw it close. The red-capped parakeet, for example, specializes in removing seeds from eucalyptus pods, which constitute a major part of its diet. When the birds find the pods on the ground, they grasp them tightly with one foot and pull the seeds out with their extremely long beak. If the parakeets pick the pods high up in a tree, they drop them to the ground to be opened there later. *Barnardius* and *Platycercus* species can even bring food to their beak with a foot.

Filing Ridges
See Bill of the Parakeet.

Flight Feathers
The quills of a bird's wing or tail that support it in flight.

Floor Grate
Many cages come equipped with a floor grate, which is intended to keep the birds from touching their droppings. However, the grate prevents the birds from pecking in the sand and picking up small stones that are essential to their digestive process. Moreover, many parakeet species enjoy playing on the floor of the cage or aviary and scratching in the sand. Often they also copulate there. For these reasons, the floor grate should be removed and the sand cleaned daily.

Exception: If a bird is sick and has to be isolated in a cage, replace the floor grate to keep the parakeet from becoming reinfected by its own droppings.

Glossary

G

Genus
Each genus consists of one species or several biologically related species and their subspecies.
Examples:
• Budgerigar:
Genus = *Melopsittacus*
Species = *Melopsittacus undulatus*
• Grass parakeets:
Genus = *Neophema*
Species = *Neophema elegans* (Pennant's parakeet), *Neophema pulchella* (turquoise parakeet), and *Neophema splendida* (scarlet-chested parakeet)
• Stanley parakeet:
Genus = *Platycercus*
Species = *Platycercus icterotis*
Subspecies = *Platycercus ic-* *terotis icterotis* (western Stanley parakeet) and *Platycercus icterotis xanthogenis* (eastern Stanley parakeet)

Geographic Subspecies
Many parakeet species have developed an astonishing number of subspecies. This is the result of geographic circumstances. The red-fronted parakeet, for example, lives in New Zealand and on many of the neighboring islands. The isolated island populations gave rise to subspecies, which, however, differ in size and plumage colors only in minor ways from the nominate form (see Nominate Form).

Geologic Age
Fossil discoveries suggest that parrots and parakeets lived on earth as long as 20 to 30 million years ago. The fossils all come from strata of the Oligocene epoch, the last third of the Tertiary period. Parrots probably also existed in Europe at that time, because a parrotlike fossil was found in these strata at Allier, France.

Gloger's Rule
The colors of parakeets' feathers are composed of green, blue, yellow, and red. Green is formed by overlaying blue and yellow, and blue is produced by the pigment melanin and refractive structures. Red and yellow are present in lipochrome, a naturally occurring pigment that contains a lipoid. The wetter the habitat of a parakeet, the greater the proportions of melanin and lipochrome become; red, blue, and black gain in intensity. The drier a region, the smaller the share of melanin and lipochrome; green and red are replaced extensively by yellow.

L

Lore
The space between the eye and the bill.

M

Medicine Chest
It is advisable to keep a small medicine chest for your parakeets, so that you can administer first aid in an emergency. This medicine chest should contain the following: Cotton swabs, tweezers, a liquid styptic, iodine, dressing gauze, Band-Aids, healing ointment, eye ointment, boric acid solution (for eye inflammations), animal charcoal (for diarrhea), paraffin oil (for constipation), and clippers, which can be used if needed to shorten claws and beaks.

Molt
Molting is not an illness, but a natural feather-shedding process by which the feathers are renewed. Parakeets customarily molt once a year, but frequent sharp fluctuations in temperature often can result in several intermediary molting periods on a smaller scale. Young birds weather the molt without any impairment of their general health. Older or weak parakeets occasionally appear to be sick during molting. If so, they will

need warmth and quiet. If necessary, use infrared light to warm them (see What to Do First, page 46).

During molting season, all parakeets need a diet that is rich in vitamins and includes fruit, vegetables, and sprouted seeds (see page 38). The birds lose a substantial number of feathers when they molt. Small feathers grow back within a few days; large ones take several weeks. Molting seldom renders a bird unable to fly, but if you see that one of your parakeets has trouble flying up from the ground, attach climbing aids—hemp ropes or branches, for example—to the feeding shelf and to the branch where it sleeps and perches.

Monogamous
Most parakeets are monogamous; that is, they form a lifelong bond with a mate of the opposite sex. The Asiatic psittaculid parakeets are an exception; they bond with a mate only during brooding season.

Mutation
Changes in a gene or chromosome that give rise to the various species of a genus. Mutations are changes that nature produces randomly, and they result in advantages or disadvantages for an individual of a species. If the changes are disadvantageous, the animal might not survive long, because it will be less equipped for the struggle to survive than other, "normal," members of its species. If the mutation creates advantages, the animal will be better able to prevail than its

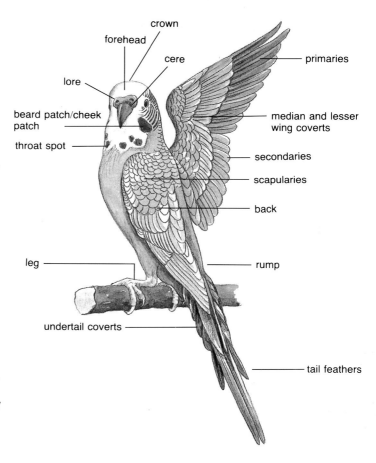

crown
forehead
cere
primaries
lore
beard patch/cheek patch
median and lesser wing coverts
throat spot
secondaries
scapularies
back
leg
rump
undertail coverts
tail feathers

fellows, and it will produce descendants equipped in turn with the acquired advantages.

N

Newcastle Disease
Newcastle disease, also called avian pseudoplague or avian pneumoencephalitis, can affect any bird. It is a dreaded viral infection, marked by symptoms that resemble those of psittaco-

sis (see page 46), usually accompanied by extreme difficulty in breathing. Affected birds need to be treated by a veterinarian. The prognosis, however, is usually poor.

Nomenclature
A set of names or terms used in a particular field of knowledge. You need to know the following about the Latin names of parakeets: The name of the genus always is given first—for

Glossary

example, *Platycercus*, the genus of the rosellas. Next comes the species name, not capitalized—for example, *Platycercus elegans* (Pennant's parakeet). If an additional lower-cased term follows, the animal in question is a subspecies.

Nominate Form
The form of a living creature that was described first.

O

Overwintering
If your parakeets live in an outdoor aviary, a heated night shelter is absolutely essential for winter. During the winter months, the temperature there should range between 44° and 48°F (7°–9°C). Most parakeet species come from tropical regions and would not survive a harsh winter. True, the temperatures in the tropics occasion-

ally do sink below 32°F (0°C) at night, but never for more than a few hours.

P

Parasites
The following parasites may occur in parakeets:

Red bird mites: They live on the parakeets' blood. During the day, the mites hide in cracks, for example, in the nest box or in the mounts of the branch perches; at night they come out and suck the birds' blood. Left unchecked, the mites will multiply and spend their daytime hours too under the parakeets' wings. Seen under a powerful magnifying glass, the mites look like tiny red or blackish dots. Affected birds fiddle nervously with their feathers and scratch frequently. This should be treated by a veterinarian. To control the mites, disinfect the enclosed area at once and use a product specifically designed to kill the parasite. Ask your veterinarian to recommend a suitable remedy.

Parakeet mange, scaly leg mite, scaly face mite, or mycosis of the beak: Also caused by a type of mite (*Cnemidocoptes pilae*). The symptoms are brownish growths on the beak and sometimes also on the cere or the legs. These start as a barely visible whitish-gray coating. Dab a preparation recommended by the veterinarian on the affected places.

Bird lice: Wingless insects that feed on skin scales and portions of feathers. They cause intense itching. The birds behave as if infested with red

bird mites. They have to be treated with a remedy recommended by a veterinarian.

Important: Don't stop the treatment too soon. The parasites lay eggs, from which new parasites hatch after a short time.

Pinion
The wing; the terminal section of the wing; the flight feathers.

Poisonous Plants
Chinese primrose, poison nut (*Strychnos nux-vomica*), old maid or Madagascar periwinkle (*Catharanthus*), Christ's thorn, all *Dieffenbachia* species, yew, hyacinth, periwinkle (*Vinca minor*), all members of the nightshade family (such as coral bush), Madagascar palm (*Pachypodium*), daffodils, oleander, berries of ardisia plants, poinsettia, croton (*Codiaeum variegatum*), snowdrop (*Ornithogalum umbellatum*), snow-on-the-mountain (*Euphorbia marginata*), ornamental asparagus berries, azaleas, wax plant (*Hoya carnosa*), members of the *Brugmansia* (formerly *Datura*) family, cyclamen, all members of the lily family—particularly *Gloriosa*, the glory lily—and all tropical house plants whose leaves are sprinkled with whitish or yellowish spots. The following plants are actually not poisonous, but secrete substances that irritate the mucous membranes and can be harmful to parakeets: Ivy, monstera (*Monstera deliciosa*), flamingo flower, meadow saffron (*Colchicum autumnale*), *Aglaonema*, philodendron, *Schefflera*.

Avoid cactuses and other

plants with thorns or spines. The birds might injure their eyes on them.

Primaries
The principal quills of the bird's wings.

Q

Quill
A large stiff feather of the wing or tail; the hollow stiff barrel of a feather.

S

Self-feeder
(Automatic Feeder)
Tube-shaped container into which the grain mix for the parakeets is placed. The food automatically drops into a small feeding trough, from which the birds peck the grain.

Advantage: Theoretically, the birds always are supplied with clean food.

Disadvantages: When using a self-feeder, you always have to check to see whether it is in working order and make sure the grains do not get stuck. Birds have been known to starve to death in front of a full feeder because the feed mechanism was blocked. Many parakeets even succeed in opening the refill valve. Then they try to creep in, and they get stuck.

Sexing
Experienced breeders determine the sex of their birds by the plumage colors, bill shape, head, or body length. Sometimes the tail marking, too,

serves as an indicator. There are parakeet species, however, whose gender cannot be determined on the basis of external features. The most foolproof method of sexing these species is endoscopy (see Endoscopy). An additional method of determining the sex is examination of the bird's droppings. The results of this examination, however, are not always conclusive.

Sexual Dimorphism
Clearly discernible difference between the sexes of a species. For example, the head of the plumhead parakeet has the color of a blue plum in the male, while it is much lighter and grayer in the female.

Species
Species is the term used to designate a group of living beings whose body structure is essentially the same. External features within a species may vary widely. The members of a species constitute a reproductive community.

Subspecies
Subspecies differ from the species by more or less conspicuous external features. If the habitats of two subspecies overlap or if they meet each other while traveling around, parakeets of two different subspecies may mate and raise so-called bastards.

Symbiosis
The mutually advantageous coexistence of dissimilar species.

T

Taking the Chicks under Her Wing
This is the term for the way the female warms her nestlings. With her plumage slightly ruffled, she sits on her young without harming them.

V

Vane
The web or flat expanded part of a feather.

Special Tips for Parakeet Breeding

Name	Body length (inches/cm)	M/F differ	Eggs	Incubation period (days)	Nestling period (weeks)
Rosellas (*Platycerus* species)					
• Stanley pkt., *P. icterotis*	10/25	yes	3–7	20	4–5
• Pennant's pkt., *P. elegans*	14/36	no	4–6	20	5
• Pale-headed rosella, *P. adscitus*	12/30	no	3–5	20	5
• Eastern rosella, *P. eximius*	12½/32	no	5–7	20	5
Red-backed pkts. (*Psephotus* species)					
• *P. haematogaster*	11/28	yes	4–7	21	5
• Mulga pkt., *P. varius*	10⅔/27	yes	4–7	21	5
• Red-rumped pkt., *P. haematonotus*	11/28	yes	4–7	17–20	4–5
Grass pkts. (*Neophema* species)					
• Elegant pkt., *N. elegans*	9/23	yes	4–6	18	4
• Blue-winged pkt., *N. chrysostoma*	8⅔/22	yes	4–6	18	4
• Turqoise pkt., *N. pulchella*	8/20	yes	4–6	18	4
• Scarlet-chested pkt., *N. splendida*	8/20	yes	3–5	18	4
Budgerigar (*Melopsittacus* species)					
• Budgerigar, *M. undulatus*	7/18	yes	4–7	18	4
Cockatiel (*Nymphicus* species)					
• cockatiel, *N. hollandicus*	12½/32	yes	4–7	21	5
Bourke's pkt. (*Neopsephotus* species)					
• Bourke's pkt., *N. bourkii*	8/20	yes	4–5	18	4
***Purpureicephalus* species**					
• Red-capped pkt., *P. spurius*	14/36	yes	4–6	20	5
***Polytelis* species**					
• Regent pkt., *P. anthopeplus*	16/40	yes	3–6	22	6
• Superb pkt., *P. swainsonii*	16/40	yes	4–6	20	5
• Princess of Wales pkt., *P. alexandrae*	18/45	yes	4–7	20	5
***Barnardius* species**					
• Port Lincoln pkt., *B. zonarius*	15/38	yes	5–6	20	5
• Malee ringneck, *B. barnardi*	13/33	yes	4–6	20	5
***Cyanoramphus* species**					
• Red-fronted N.Z. pkt., *C. novaezelandiae*	11/28	yes	5–9	20	5
• Yellow-fronted N.Z. pkt., *C. auriceps*	9/23	yes	5–9	19	5
Quaker pkt. (*Myiopsitta* species)					
• Quaker pkt., *M. monachus*	11½/29	no	5–8	26	6
***Brotogeris* species**					
• Canary-winged pkt., *B. versicolorus chiriri*	9/23	no	5–6	23	7
***Aratinga* species**					
• Mitred conure, *A. mitrata*	15/38	no	3–4	23	7
***Nandayus* species**					
• Nanday pkt., *N. nenday*	12½/32	no	4–5	26	6–7
***Psittacula* species**					
• Ringneck pkt., *P. krameri*	16/40	yes	3–6	23	6
• Plumhead pkt., *P. cyanocephala*	14/35	yes	4–6	23	7
• Mustached pkt., *P. alexandri fasciata*	13/33	yes	3–4	28	7

...berty (...nths)	Nest box (L × W × H in inches/cm)	Entry hole (diameter in inches/cm)	Leg band (mm)
...–18	10x10x20(25x25x50)	2⅓/6	5.0
...24	10⅔x10⅔x24(27x27x60)	3/8	6.0
...12	10x10x24(25x25x60)	3/8	5.5
...12	10x10x24(25x25x60)	2¾/7	5.5
...–9	8x8x24(20x20x60)	2¾/7	5.5
...–9	8x8x14(20x20x35)	2¾/7	4.5
...–9	10x10x14(25x25x35)	2¾/7	4.5
...–12	8x8x12(20x20x30)	2⅓/6	4.0
...–12	8x8x20(20x20x50)	2⅓/6	4.0
...–12	8x8x20(20x20x50)	2/5	4.0
...–9	6x6x12(15x15x30)	2/5	4.0
6	10x6x8(25x15x20)	2/5	4.2
9	12x10x10(30x25x25)	2¾/7	5.5
5	6x6x18(15x15x45)	2⅓/6	4.0
...–18	12x12x20(30x30x50)	3/7–8	5.5
...–24	11x11x28(28x28x70)	3½/8–10	6.5
...–24	10x10x28(25x25x70)	3/8	6.5
...–24	10x10x28(25x25x70)	3/8	5.5
...–18	14x14x28(35x35x70)	3½/9	6.0
...–18	12x12x28(30x30x70)	3/8	6.0
...–9	8x8x18(20x20x45)	2⅓/6	4.5
6	8x8x16(20x20x40)	2/5	4.5
12	12x12x16(30x30x40)	2¾/7	6.0
...–12	7x7x16(18x18x40)	2¾/7	4.5
12	12x12x24(30x30x60)	3½/9	6.5
...–12	12x12x16(30x30x40)	2¾/7	6.0
...–30	12x12x20(30x30x50)	3½/9	7.0
...–30	8x8x12(20x20x30)	3/8	5.5
...–30	8x10x20(20x25x50)	3/8	5.5

Hatching is extremely hard work for a young bird. With the help of its egg tooth, it frees itself from the egg.

This budgerigar nestling is 10 to 12 days old. Its eyes are open and the quills on its wings, tail, and head are already beginning to sprout.

This budgerigar is now about three weeks old. All its down feathers are fully developed. Soon it can leave the nest box and fly.

Index

Boldface type indicates color plates.

BARRON'S BOOKS FOR DOG OWNERS

Barron's offers a wonderful variety of books for dog owners and prospective owners, all written by experienced breeders, trainers, veterinarians, or qualified experts on canines. Most books are heavily illustrated with handsome color photos and instructive line art. They'll tell you facts you need to know, and give you advice on purchasing, feeding, grooming, training, and keeping a healthy pet.

Before You Buy That Puppy
ISBN 0-8120-1750-1
The Book of the Mixed Breed Dog
ISBN 0-7641-5065-0
Careers With Dogs
ISBN 0-7641-0503-5
Caring for Your Older Dog
ISBN 0-8120-9149-3
Civilizing Your Puppy, 2nd Ed.
ISBN 0-8120-9787-4
Communicating With Your Dog
ISBN 0-7641-0758-5
Compatible Canines
ISBN 0-7641-0724-0
The Complete Book of Dog Breeding
ISBN 0-8120-9604-5
The Complete Book of Dog Care
ISBN 0-8120-4158-5
The Complete Guide to the Dog
ISBN 0-7641-5204-1
The Dog: A Child's Friend
ISBN 0-7641-0302-4

The Dog Care Manual
ISBN 0-8120-9163-9
The Dog Owner's Question and Answer Book
ISBN 0-7641-0647-3
Dogs from A to Z: A Dictionary of Canine Terms
ISBN 0-7641-0158-7
Educating Your Dog
ISBN 0-8120-9592-8
Encyclopedia of Dog Breeds
ISBN 0-7641-5097-9
Fun and Games With Your Dog
ISBN 0-8120-9721-1
Healthy Dog, Happy Dog: A Complete Guide to Dog Diseases and Their Treatments
ISBN 0-8120-1842-7
How to Teach Your Old Dog New Tricks
ISBN 0-8120-4544-0
Hunting Dogs from Around the World
ISBN 0-8120-6632-4

Natural Health Care for Your Dog
ISBN 0-7641-0122-6
101 Questions Your Dog Would Ask
ISBN 0-7641-0886-7
Pudgy Pooch, Picky Pooch
ISBN 0-7641-0289-3
Puppies
ISBN 0-8120-6631-6
Saved! A Guide to Success With Your Shelter Dog
ISBN 0-7641-0062-9
Show Me!
ISBN 0-8120-9710-6
Train Your Dog
ISBN 0-7641-0967-7
The Trick is in the Training
ISBN 0-7641-0492-6
The Well-Behaved Dog
ISBN 0-7641-5066-9

Barron's Educational Series, Inc.
250 Wireless Blvd., Hauppauge, NY 11788 • To order toll-free: 1-800-645-3476
In Canada: Georgetown Book Warehouse • 34 Armstrong Ave., Georgetown, Ont. L7G 4R9
Order toll-free in Canada: 1-800-247-7160
Or order from your favorite bookstore or pet store
Visit our web site at: www.barronseduc.com

(#111) 9/99

Barron's Books for Fish Enthusiasts

Barron's offers a wide variety of books for fish enthusiasts, fish hobbyists, and prospective owners looking for more information. All have been written by experienced breeders or qualified experts on fish - and most are heavily illustrated with handsome color photos and instructive line art. They'll tell you what you need to know about the care, environment, and feeding of your aquatic friends.

OWNER'S MANUALS

Cichlids
ISBN 0-8120-4597-1

Clownfish and Sea Anemones
ISBN 0-7641-0511-6

Discus Fish
ISBN 0-8120-4669-2

Freshwater Stingrays
ISBN 0-7641-0897-2

Goldfish
ISBN 0-8120-9016-0

Guppies, Mollies, Platys
ISBN 0-8120-1497-9

Killifish
ISBN 0-8120-4475-4

Koi
ISBN 0-8120-3568-2

Lake Tanganyika Cichlids
ISBN 0-7641-0615-5

Piranhas
ISBN 0-8120-9916-8

Tropical Fish
ISBN 0-8120-4700-1

Your First Marine Aquarium
ISBN 0-7641-0447-0

HANDBOOKS

The New Aquarium Fish Handbook
ISBN 0-8120-3682-4

The New Saltwater Aquarium Handbook
ISBN 0-8120-4482-7

REFERENCE

Adventure Aquarium
ISBN 0-7641-0300-8

Aquarium Fish
ISBN 0-8120-1350-6

Family Pet Series: Aquarium Fish
ISBN 0-7641-5084-7

Aquarium Fish Breeding
ISBN 0-8120-4474-6

The Aquarium Fish Survival Manual
ISBN 0-8120-9391-7

Aquarium Plants Manual
ISBN 0-8120-1687-4

Goldfish and Ornamental Carp
ISBN 0-8120-9286-4

Labyrinth Fish
ISBN 0-8120-5635-3

The Marine Reef Aquarium Handbook
ISBN 0-8120-9598-7

North American Native Fishes for the Home Aquarium
ISBN 0-7641-0367-9

The Tropical Marine Fish Survival Manual
ISBN 0-8120-9372-0

Barron's Educational Series, Inc.
250 Wireless Blvd., Hauppauge, NY 11788
To order toll-free: 1-800-645-3476
In Canada: Georgetown Book Warehouse,
34 Armstrong Ave., Georgetown, Ont. L7G 4R9
Order toll-free in Canada: 1-800-247-7160
Or order from your favorite bookstore or pet store
Visit our web site at: www.barronseduc.com

(65a) 9/99

Useful Addresses and Literature

United States

American Federation of Aviculture (AFA)
P.O. Box 1568
Redondo Beach, California 90278

Association of Avian Veterinarians
P.O. Box 211720
Boca Raton, Florida 33481

Avicultural Society of America, Inc.
8228 Sulphur Road
Ojai, California 93023

National Parrot Association
8 North Hoffman Lane
Hauppauge, New York 11788

The Society of Parrot Breeders and Exhibitors

Great Britain

The Avicultural Society
Warren Hill, Halford's Lane
Hartley Wintney, Hampshire RG27 8AG

The European Aviculture Council
P.O. Box 74
Bury St. Edmunds, Suffolk IP30 OHS

National Council for Aviculture
87 Winn Road
Lee, London SE12 9EY

Canada

The Canadian Avicultural Society
32 Dronmore Court
Willodale, Ontario M2R 2H5

Canadian Parrot Association
Pine Oaks R.R. #3
St. Catharines, Ontario L2R 6P9

Australia

The Avicultural Society of Australia
52 Harris Road
Elliminyt, Victoria 3249

New Zealand

Avicultural Society of N.Z., Inc.
P.O. Box 21
403 Henderson, Auckland

Books

Forshaw, J., *Australian Parrots*, 2nd edition. Landsdowne Edition, 1981.

——, *Parrots of the World*, 3rd edition. Landsdowne Edition, 1989.

Kolar, Kurt, *Parrots*, Barron's Educational Series, Inc., Hauppauge, New York, 1990.

LaRosa, Don, *How to Build Everything You Need for Your Birds*, Audubon Publishing Company, Smithtown, New York, 1983.

Low, Rosemary, *The Complete Book of Parrots*, Barron's Educational Series, Inc., Hauppauge, New York, 1989.

Vriends, Matthew M., *Conures*, Barron's Educational Series, Inc., Hauppauge, New York, 1992

——, *The New Australian Parakeet Handbook*, Barron's Educational Series, Inc., Hauppauge, New York, 1992.

——, *The New Bird Handbook*, Barron's Educational Series, Inc., Hauppauge, New York, 1989.

——, *The New Cockatiel Handbook*, Barron's Educational Series, Inc., Hauppauge, New York, 1989.

Magazines

American Cage Bird Magazine
One Glamore Court
Smithtown, New York 11787

The A.F.A. Watchbird
P.O. Box 56218
Phoenix, Arizona 85079-6218

Bird Talk
P.O. Box 6050
Mission Viejo, California 92690

Bird World
P.O. Box 70
N. Hollywood, California 91603

Cage and Aviary Birds
Prospect House
9-13 Ewell Road
Cheam, Surrey SM1 499 England

Acknowledgments

The author and the publisher wish to thank Reinhard Hahn for his advice on species conservation issues, Dr. Kurt Kolar and Philipp Kramer for reading the manuscript, and Dr. Gabriele Wiesner for her advice on veterinary medicine.

The Author

Annette Wolter, an expert on birds, has many years of experience in keeping small and large parrots. She is also the successful author of Barron's pet owner's manuals on cockatiels, parrots, and parakeets.

Important Note:
This book deals with the keeping and care of parakeets.

People who are allergic to feathers or feather dust should not keep birds. If in doubt, consult your doctor before acquiring a bird.

In dealing with parakeets, you may be bitten or scratched. Have such injuries treated by a doctor at once.

"Parrot fever" (psittacosis, ornithosis) now is quite rare among parakeets (see page 46), but in some cases it can cause life-threatening symptoms in humans and parakeets. If in doubt, take your parakeet to a veterinarian (see page 46). If you have cold or flu symptoms, see your own doctor without fail. Be sure to tell the doctor that you keep birds.

Cover photos
Front cover: Eastern rosellas.
Inside front cover: Sharp-tailed conure.
Inside back cover: Eastern rosellas.
Back cover: Derbyan parakeet.

Photo credits
Angermayer/Ziesler: inside front cover; Arendt and
Schweiger: pages 8 left and right, 9, 28, 52, 53 left and
right; Coleman/Bauer: page 14; Coleman/Evans: pages 20,
21; Coleman/Prenzel: page 73 left; Coleman/Reinhard:
page 25; Coleman/Rivarola: page 37; Gröger: page 61,
back cover; Jacana/Frédéric: page 17; Jacana/Labat: page
72; Jacana/Varin: page 79 right; König: page 57; Mayer:
pages 69 left, 78 left; Okapia/Reinhard: page 69 right;
Pfeffer: page 70 left, inside back cover; Reinhard: pages
68, 75 right, 77, 78 right, 80 left and right, 81; Scholtz:
front cover, pages 7, 11, 45, 49, 66 right and left, 67 right
and left, 70 right, 71 right and left, 73 right, 74 right and
left, 75 left, 76 left, 79 left; Silvestris/A.N.T.: pages 2, 5,
32, 40, 65; Silvestris/Hosking: page 76 right.

English translation © Copyright 1992
by Barron's Educational Series, Inc.

© Copyright 1991 by Gräfe and Unzer Verlag
GmbH, Munich, Germany
The title of the German book is *Sittiche*.

Translated from the German by Kathleen Luft

All inquiries should be addressed to:
Barron's Educational Series, Inc.
250 Wireless Boulevard
Hauppauge, NY 11788

Library of Congress Catalog Card No. 92-16835

International Standard Book No. 0-8120-1351-4

Library of Congress Cataloging-In-Publication Data

Wolter, Annette.
    [Sittiche richtig pflegen und verstehen.   English]
    Long-tailed parakeets : how to take care of them and
understand them / Annete Wolter ; with 50 color photos
and drawings by György Jankovics ; consulting editor,
Mathew M. Vriends.
        p.   cm.
    Translation of: Sittiche richtig pflegen und verstenhen.
    Includes index.
    ISBN 0-8120-1351-4
1. Australian parakeets. I. Jankovics, György.
II. Vriends, Matthew M., 1937– . III. Title.
    SF473.A88W6513 1992
    636.6′865—dc20   92-16835
                                  CIP

PRINTED IN HONG KONG
45 4900 98